Philosophy

a visual encyclopedia

Philosophy

a visual encyclopedia

DK

Consultant Will Buckingham

Written by Dr. Robert Fletcher, Dr. Paola Romero,
Marianne Talbot, Nigel Warburton, Dr. Amna Whiston

DK London

Senior Editors Sam Atkinson, Pauline Savage
Senior Art Editors Louise Dick, Jacqui Swan
Editor Amanda Wyatt
Editorial Assistant Zaina Budaly
Illustrators Alejandro at KJA Artists, Eglé Každailyté and
Giordano Poloni at Agency Rush
US Editor Jenny Wilson
US Executive Editor Lori Cates Hand
Managing Editor Lisa Gillespie
Managing Art Editor Owen Peyton Jones
Production Editor Robert Dunn
Senior Production Controller Meskerem Berhane
Jacket Design Development Manager Sophia MTT
Publisher Andrew Macintyre
Associate Publishing Director Liz Wheeler
Art Director Karen Self
Publishing Director Jonathan Metcalf

DK Delhi

Senior Editor Shatarupa Chaudhuri
Senior Art Editor Vikas Chauhan
Project Art Editor Heena Sharma
Art Editors Tanisha Mandal, Debjyoti Mukherjee
Illustrator Sanya Jain
Assistant Editor Sai Prasanna
Managing Editor Kingshuk Ghoshal
Managing Art Editor Govind Mittal
Picture Researcher Geetika Bhandari
Picture Research Manager Taiyaba Khatoon
DTP Designers Nand Kishor Acharya, Anita Yadav
Pre-production Manager Balwant Singh
Production Manager Pankaj Sharma
Senior Jacket Designer Suhita Dharamjit

First American Edition, 2020
Published in the United States by DK Publishing
1450 Broadway, Suite 801, New York, NY 10018

A catalog record for this book
is available from the Library of Congress.
ISBN 978-0-7440-2000-7 (Paperback)
ISBN 978-0-7440-2912-3 (Hardcover)

DK books are available at special discounts when purchased in
bulk for sales promotions, premiums, fund-raising, or educational
use. For details, contact: DK Publishing Special Markets,
1450 Broadway, Suite 801, New York, NY 10018
SpecialSales@dk.com

Printed and bound in UAE

For the curious
www.dk.com

Contents

About this book

Throughout history, people have wondered about the world around them and their own place in it. They have puzzled over what is real. They have discussed what it means to know and believe things. They have argued about the nature of truth. They have asked what it means to lead a good life. And through wondering about all these things, they have tried to understand the world more fully. Philosophy is about asking these big questions about life, so that we can deepen our understanding and act more wisely.

The Thinker, **by French sculptor Auguste Rodin**

A LOVE OF WISDOM

Whenever people look at the world with fresh eyes, think things through more clearly, and ask new questions, they are practicing philosophy. The word "philosophy" comes from a Greek word meaning "the love of wisdom." But although the word is Greek, philosophy happens all over the world, and in very different civilizations. In some cultures philosophers have always written their ideas down, while in others ideas have been passed on by word of mouth. There are many separate traditions of philosophy around the world.

DIFFERENT TRADITIONS

Some of the world's major philosophical traditions are found in India, China, and across Europe and the Middle East. Philosophers such as Siddhārtha Gautama in India, Confucius in China, Ibn Sīnā in Persia, and many ancient Greek thinkers, have left a strong mark on history. Their thinking has shaped the cultures of Asia, Europe, and beyond. But philosophy is not limited to these traditions. It happens wherever people wonder about the world around them.

The founder of Buddhism in India, Siddhārtha Gautama

The ancient Greek thinker Anaximander

The Muslim Arab philosopher Ibn Sīnā

The Chinese teacher Confucius

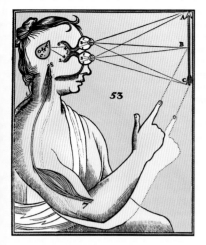

Illustration by René Descartes examining the relationship between the mind's power to reason and the body's ability to move

REASONING ABOUT REASON

All the different branches of human knowledge use reasoning (the ability to think things through) to understand the world. Sciences such as physics, chemistry, and biology combine observation, experiment, and reasoning to understand the natural world. But what makes philosophers different is that they often step back to ask questions that scientists don't ask: What is reason? What does it mean to understand? Philosophers don't just use reason as a tool. They go further, and even reason about the ability to reason itself.

PHILOSOPHY AND BELIEF

The world's cultures are rich in the traditions of myth and religion. These belief systems, like philosophy, can help people to make sense of their place in the world and decide what is right and wrong. Reason plays a part in many religions, but beliefs are often viewed as matters of faith—they are taken on trust. Philosophers must rely on reason alone to investigate beliefs.

Traditional Yoruba religious dance

THOUGHT EXPERIMENTS

Philosophers use many methods to explore the questions they are interested in. One tool that they often use is a thought experiment. This involves creating an imaginary scenario that allows them to fully explore a problem. Throughout this book, wherever you see a question mark inside a thought bubble close to an illustration, a philosopher is asking you to "imagine" a particular scenario as a thought experiment, to help you think a philosophical problem through.

Brain in a vat thought experiment

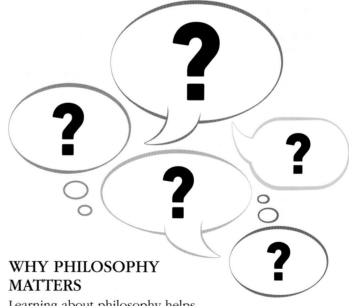

WHY PHILOSOPHY MATTERS

Learning about philosophy helps people to think and reason more clearly. It encourages you to ask deeper questions about the world. It gives insights into your own culture and its traditions, and the cultures and traditions of others. And it can help you find your own solutions to the question of what it means to lead a good life.

PHILOSOPHY THROUGH THE AGES
700 BCE – 250 CE

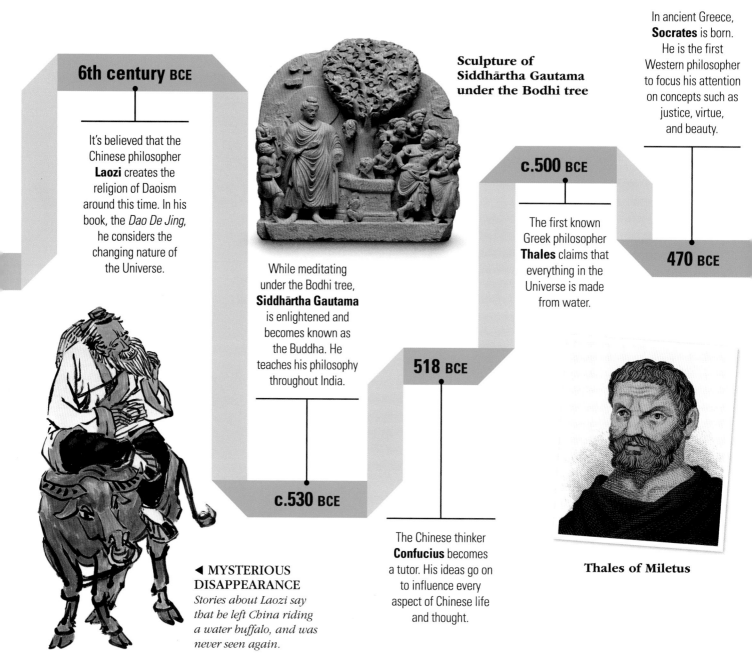

6th century BCE

It's believed that the Chinese philosopher **Laozi** creates the religion of Daoism around this time. In his book, the *Dao De Jing*, he considers the changing nature of the Universe.

Sculpture of Siddhārtha Gautama under the Bodhi tree

While meditating under the Bodhi tree, **Siddhārtha Gautama** is enlightened and becomes known as the Buddha. He teaches his philosophy throughout India.

In ancient Greece, **Socrates** is born. He is the first Western philosopher to focus his attention on concepts such as justice, virtue, and beauty.

c.500 BCE

The first known Greek philosopher **Thales** claims that everything in the Universe is made from water.

470 BCE

518 BCE

c.530 BCE

◄ **MYSTERIOUS DISAPPEARANCE**
Stories about Laozi say that he left China riding a water buffalo, and was never seen again.

The Chinese thinker **Confucius** becomes a tutor. His ideas go on to influence every aspect of Chinese life and thought.

Thales of Miletus

People have always asked questions about the nature of the Universe, the point of existence, and what makes a person "good." In very ancient times, answers were found in folklore, myth, and legend. But around 2,800 years ago, people started to change how they thought about their world. Instead of looking for answers in stories of gods and heroes they looked for explanations using their ability to reason.

Some scholars have called this important period the "Axial Age," because it was a time when people's ideas about their place in the Universe shifted or turned, in the same way that a wheel turns on its axis. It was during the Axial Age, which lasted from the 8th to the 3rd centuries BCE, that many of the world's major philosophical traditions began to emerge across China, India, and Mediterranean Europe.

The Greek philosopher **Zeno of Elea** questions the nature of change through a series of paradoxes—logical puzzles that appear to lead to absurd conclusions.

c.490–425 BCE

Zeno of Elea

◄ **THE DIVINE TEACHER**
In the Bhagavad Gita, *the god Krishna encourages Prince Arjuna to do his duty as a warrior by fighting in a just war.*

c.400 BCE

In ancient India, believers in Hinduism compose the **Bhagavad Gita**, a poetic story that teaches the importance of duty.

c.399–390 BCE

The Greek philosopher **Plato** writes a series of dialogues (conversations) that explore philosophical ideas.

335 BCE

A student of Plato, **Aristotle**, opens a philosophy school known as the Lyceum. His methods go on to form the foundations of Western science.

Painting of Aristotle's Lyceum

Philosophy begins in wonder.
PLATO, *Theaetetus* (4th century BCE)

There are many reasons why philosophy developed, but two of the most important were the growth of cities and the expansion of trade. As cities grew and began to trade, humans began to interact with each other like never before. People were exposed to different ways of thinking, and societies became more complicated. The ideas that people had about the world had to develop to keep up with this new complexity.

This period produced some of history's greatest thinkers: Confucius in China, Siddhārtha Gautama in India, and Socrates, Plato, and Aristotle in Greece. The ideas of these ancient philosophers were so powerful that they laid the foundations for the cultures that followed them, and their influence continued to be felt centuries after their deaths. The questions they asked still preoccupy philosophers today, more than 2,000 years later.

PHILOSOPHY THROUGH THE AGES

250–1400

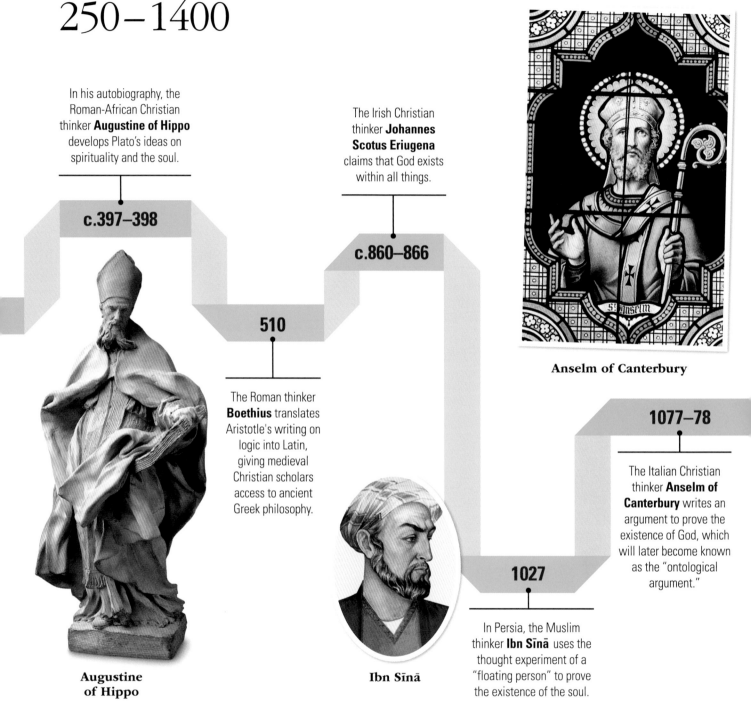

In his autobiography, the Roman-African Christian thinker **Augustine of Hippo** develops Plato's ideas on spirituality and the soul.

c.397–398

The Irish Christian thinker **Johannes Scotus Eriugena** claims that God exists within all things.

c.860–866

510

The Roman thinker **Boethius** translates Aristotle's writing on logic into Latin, giving medieval Christian scholars access to ancient Greek philosophy.

Anselm of Canterbury

1077–78

The Italian Christian thinker **Anselm of Canterbury** writes an argument to prove the existence of God, which will later become known as the "ontological argument."

1027

In Persia, the Muslim thinker **Ibn Sīnā** uses the thought experiment of a "floating person" to prove the existence of the soul.

Augustine of Hippo

Ibn Sīnā

In the early centuries of the 1st millennium CE, the power of the Roman Empire declined in Europe. At the same time, a new religion was spreading across the continent—Christianity. In 313 CE, the practice of this new religion was permitted throughout the Roman Empire by Emperor Constantine.

The spread of Christianity across Europe began in the Greek-speaking lands around the Mediterranean. The original language of the Bible's New Testament is Greek, and Christianity was heavily influenced by ancient Greek philosophy. However, some of the earliest Christian thinkers, such as Augustine of Hippo, struggled to connect ideas found in Greek philosophy with Christian teachings, as they seemed to be very different.

As the Roman Empire collapsed, Western Europe became politically divided. Cities and small states were constantly at war with one another, and there was little time for philosophy. However, in the Middle East, a new

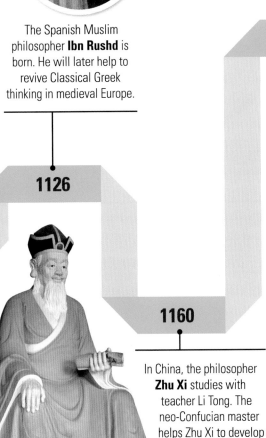

Ibn Rushd

> I do not seek to **understand in order** to believe, but **believe** in order that I might **understand**.
>
> ANSELM OF CANTERBURY, *Proslogion* (1077–1078)

The Italian Christian **Thomas Aquinas** writes the *Summa Theologiae*, a detailed guide to Christian teachings that is still used by the Catholic Church today.

1190

The Spanish Muslim philosopher **Ibn Rushd** is born. He will later help to revive Classical Greek thinking in medieval Europe.

The Spanish thinker **Moses Maimonides** completes *The Guide for the Perplexed*, bringing together his Jewish beliefs with the writings of Aristotle. In this book he argues that the essence of God is unknowable.

1265

1126

Thomas Aquinas

1160

In China, the philosopher **Zhu Xi** studies with teacher Li Tong. The neo-Confucian master helps Zhu Xi to develop his own principles of neo-Confucianism, known as *daoxue*.

c.1300

A page from *The Guide for the Perplexed*

The English philosopher **William of Ockham** develops a principle that will come to be known as "Ockham's razor," which says that the best possible explanation is often the simplest.

Zhu Xi

religion—Islam—was emerging, making huge contributions to the development of philosophy.

Between the 8th and the 14th centuries, Islam experienced a golden age. The city of Baghdad in modern-day Iraq became a center of philosophy, where philosophers worked to translate ancient Greek texts into Arabic. Later, Arabic texts were translated into Latin, the language of scholars in Europe at the time. These translations had a huge impact on Christian beliefs.

Buddhism was introduced into China from India around the 2nd century CE. It gained popularity and widely influenced Chinese culture, transforming approaches to poetry and art. In 618 CE China came under the rule of the Tang dynasty, and Buddhism was included among the local Chinese traditions of Daoism and Confucianism as one of the three main religions and philosophies ("three teachings") of the Chinese-speaking world.

PHILOSOPHY THROUGH THE AGES

1400–1850

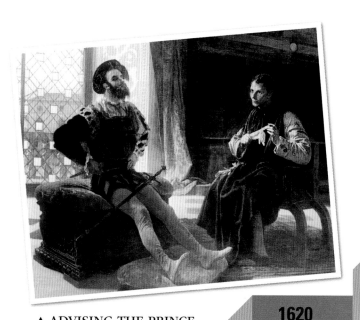

▲ ADVISING THE PRINCE
Machiavelli advised the 16th-century Italian ruler Lorenzo de' Medici on political tactics.

Thomas Hobbes

The English thinker **Thomas Hobbes** argues that a ruler with absolute power is needed to maintain order and stability among the people.

1637

The French philosopher and scientist **René Descartes** makes the now famous statement *"cogito, ergo sum"* ("I think therefore I am").

1620

1651

1532

The political book *The Prince* by Italian thinker **Niccolò Machiavelli** is published. It instructs political leaders on how best to govern.

The English philosopher **Francis Bacon** writes *Novum Organum*, which sets out his ideas on scientific methods. These go on to form the basis of modern science.

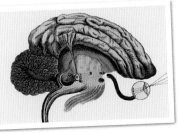

◄ PROCESS OF SIGHT
Descartes made illustrations, such as this drawing of the process of sight, to accompany his writings.

In the 14th century, Italian scholars began to study ancient Greek and Roman writings that had been brought to Italy from the Byzantine Empire to the east. This led to a "renaissance" (rebirth) of wisdom and learning in Europe over the following centuries. During the Renaissance, people started to reject the medieval Christian teachings that had dominated their lives, and instead embraced new approaches to education and philosophy. Philosophers started to think more deeply about *humanitas* ("human nature"), rather than focusing on questions about God.

The Renaissance was a time of great technological and political change in Europe. The development of a new kind of printing press by Johannes Gutenberg enabled books containing revolutionary ideas to be printed more quickly and distributed more widely.

Also around this time, European nations began to explore the world by sea, looking to trade and plunder. Traditionally, the Christian Church had been important to European states because it had lots of money, but as nations grew richer, the Church's wealth mattered less and its power weakened further. The discovery of new sea routes to Asia also brought Europeans into contact with philosophical traditions from the East. Ancient texts from China and India were translated into European languages, introducing fresh ideas to Western thought.

> # It is necessary that at least once in your life, you **doubt**, as far as possible, **all things**.
>
> RENÉ DESCARTES, *Principles of Philosophy* (1644)

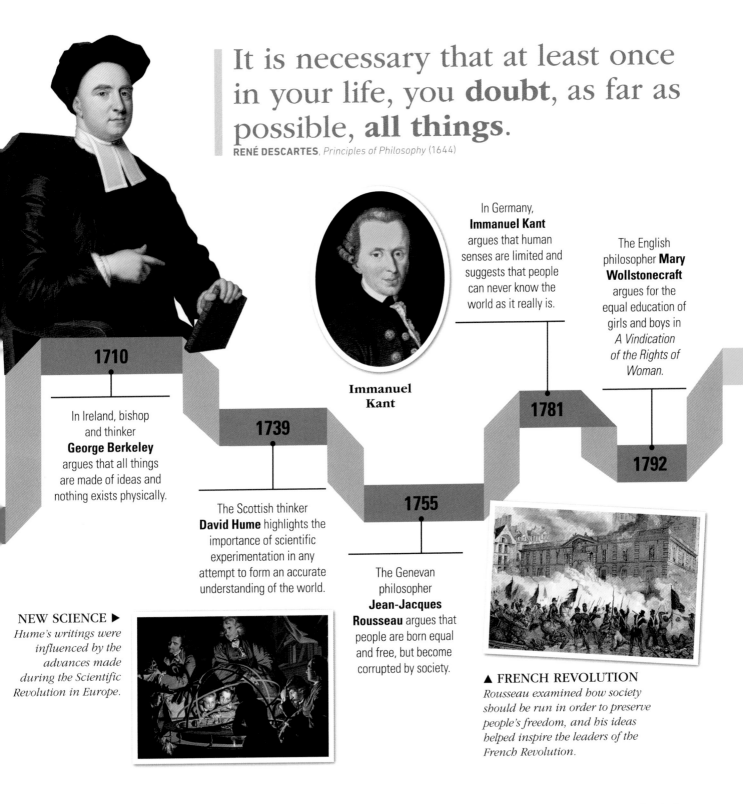

1710

In Ireland, bishop and thinker **George Berkeley** argues that all things are made of ideas and nothing exists physically.

1739

The Scottish thinker **David Hume** highlights the importance of scientific experimentation in any attempt to form an accurate understanding of the world.

Immanuel Kant

In Germany, **Immanuel Kant** argues that human senses are limited and suggests that people can never know the world as it really is.

1755

The Genevan philosopher **Jean-Jacques Rousseau** argues that people are born equal and free, but become corrupted by society.

The English philosopher **Mary Wollstonecraft** argues for the equal education of girls and boys in *A Vindication of the Rights of Woman.*

1781

1792

NEW SCIENCE ▶
Hume's writings were influenced by the advances made during the Scientific Revolution in Europe.

▲ FRENCH REVOLUTION
Rousseau examined how society should be run in order to preserve people's freedom, and his ideas helped inspire the leaders of the French Revolution.

Toward the end of the Renaissance, the Scientific Revolution (1543–1687) began to spread across Europe. The growth of science led people to think about the world in new ways, inspiring a philosophical movement known as the Enlightenment, which reached its height in the 1700s. During the Enlightenment, thinkers argued for the importance of reasoning.

Meanwhile in India, many philosophers were influenced by Western thought. Studying Western philosophy gave Indian philosophers different ways of approaching Indian philosophical traditions. This led to what is sometimes called the "Indian Renaissance," with philosophers such as Ram Mohan Roy developing new ideas about ancient Indian philosophy.

During this period, China traded with Europe, which brought Chinese thinkers into closer contact with Western thought. But Confucianism was little changed by these imported ideas, and remained one of the most important philosophies in China. Scholars such as Wang Yangming developed Confucian values in new ways.

PHILOSOPHY THROUGH THE AGES

1850–present

The English philosopher **John Stuart Mill** promotes women's suffrage, presenting a petition to the British parliament.

1866

J.S. Mill argued for women's right to vote

Friedrich Nietzsche

The German thinker **Friedrich Nietzsche** introduces the idea of the *Übermensch* ("Superman") —a person who relies on their own abilities to change the world for the better.

1883–1885

1867

The German philosopher **Karl Marx** writes *Capital*, which describes how workers will gain power in the political movement known as communism.

1903

In the US, **Charles Sanders Peirce** delivers a series of lectures at Harvard University, arguing that philosophical theories should have practical uses.

▼ FLYING THE FLAG
The writings of Karl Marx supported and influenced the rise of communism.

In the mid-19th century, philosophers in Europe, including the great German thinkers Friedrich Nietzsche and Karl Marx, introduced new ideas that were fiercely in opposition to Christian thinking and challenged the political systems of their time. Their philosophies often had the aim of changing society, and the practical effects of their ideas were felt throughout the following century.

In the US, a more practical approach to philosophy also became popular. Some American thinkers, known as pragmatists, wanted to promote philosophical ideas that were useful in daily life, rather than abstract

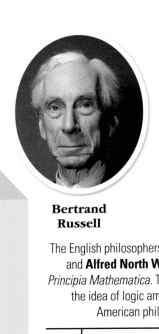

Bertrand Russell

Alfred North Whitehead

The English philosophers **Bertrand Russell** and **Alfred North Whitehead** write *Principia Mathematica*. This book popularizes the idea of logic among British and American philosophers.

1910–1913

1943

The French philosopher **Jean-Paul Sartre** writes about the purpose of existence in his book *Being and Nothingness*.

1937

The Japanese philosopher **Watsuji Tetsurō** criticizes Western ideas on ethics and instead emphasizes the importance of community.

1949

In her groundbreaking feminist book, *The Second Sex*, the French philosopher **Simone de Beauvoir** analyzes the unequal treatment of women in a male-dominated society.

▲ RISE OF FEMINISM
Simone de Beauvoir's philosophy inspired the feminist protests of the 1960s and 1970s.

1984

In science, the English philosopher **Mary Warnock** sets the ethical standards for research on human embryos.

Mary Warnock

> The philosophers have only interpreted the **world in various ways**. The point, however, is to **change it**.
>
> **KARL MARX**, *Theses on Feuerbach* (1888)

theories that could never be proved. The pragmatists preferred not to ask, "Is this idea true?," but instead, "Is this idea useful?"

From the early 1900s, philosophers started to examine how the subject of philosophy itself works. In Britain, this led to the tradition of analytic philosophy. This approach uses the tools of logic and the philosophy of language to break complex philosophical problems down into parts and analyze how they fit together. In continental Europe, many philosophers preferred to synthesize (combine) different ideas together, to explore the nature of human experience and the purpose of existence.

More recently, philosophers have looked at the similarities and differences between philosophical traditions from around the world. This study is known as comparative philosophy. Thinkers in China, for example, are interested in exploring the writings of Aristotle to understand their own traditions.

Some modern-day philosophers believe that we need to look beyond just a few "popular traditions," such as the philosophies of India, China, Europe, and North America. They are exploring philosophical traditions from elsewhere, such as Africa and South America, to discover new ways of asking and answering some of the oldest questions in human existence.

REALITY AND EXISTENCE

Philosophy began with people asking questions about the world and about their place in it. Moving away from myths and legends, philosophers found other ways of explaining what the Universe is made of and how it works, what is real, and the meaning of personal identity. These discussions came together to form the foundation of the branch of philosophy known as metaphysics.

What is everything made of?

Although we now think of it as answerable by science, the question of what all things are made of was once a philosophical one—the answer could only be debated. The early Greek philosophers had no way of testing their theories, but their views on this question closely anticipated modern-day science.

JARGON BUSTER

Substance In philosophy, something that can exist without depending on anything else.

Fundamental principle The substance or substances from which all things are made.

Pre-Socratic Greek philosophy before Socrates, or philosophy unaffected by his work.

As far as we know, Thales, from the Greek city of Miletus in Ionia (in modern-day Turkey), was the first Western philosopher to ask what everything is made of—or in philosophical terms, what is the fundamental principle. Thales lived in the 6th century BCE, well before the influential Greek thinker Socrates (see p.45). Thales's answer was that there was just one substance (a view called monism), and that this single substance was water. The idea that water could also be such things as fire and air, which don't have a watery nature, now seems strange.

> The early Greeks were the first to devise an atomic theory. Their ideas were explored by scientists in the 1700s.

Thales's pupil, Anaximander, thought that the substance all things are made of was not water, but a single material he called *apeiron*. This was something infinite, ageless, permanently in motion, and without any definite qualities. However, a pupil of Anaximander, Anaximenes, thought that *apeiron* did have a particular character, which was air. Anaximenes claimed that air could be compressed

ONE SUBSTANCE
Some pre-Socratic Greek philosophers thought that there was only one substance in the world, from which all things were made. They had different views on what that fundamental principle was.

Apeiron (meaning "the limitless" in ancient Greek) was **Anaximander's** term for the **fundamental principle**. Everything was made from it, and returned to it when destroyed.

Thales noticed **water** all around him in oceans, in rivers, and in rain. He realized that it was **vital** to every living thing, so it seemed rational that everything in the Universe was made from it.

to take on different appearances and qualities, such as water and earth. Towards the end of the 6th century BCE, Heraclitus, another Ionian Greek, thought that the fundamental principle was fire. Just as the flames of a fire seem to dance, he thought that everything is in flux—continually changing.

A different group of philosophers, led by Parmenides, were based in the Greek city of Elea in southern Italy. Like the Milesians, these thinkers also believed there was only one fundamental principle, but that it was unchanging and continuous. Parmenides' student, Zeno, argued that the opposite view (pluralism—the belief that there are many types of thing) involved absurdities, or paradoxes (see pp.92–93).

MORE THAN ONE THING
Empedocles of Acragas in Sicily, writing in the 5th century BCE, believed that the Universe was made not of one thing, but four: fire, water, earth, and air. He also described forces for change—love, which unified these four basic components, and strife, which could separate them. The basic substances could combine to form compounds with different properties. This view of compounds and their properties is similar to the science of modern chemistry.

THE WORLD IS MADE OF ATOMS
Later in the same century, the thinking of Empedocles was developed further by fellow Greeks Leucippus and Democritus, known as the Atomists. They believed that everything in the world was made up of atoms in constant motion. In their view, "atoms" were simply things that could not be split. Atoms themselves had no properties but, in combination with other atoms, they took on particular characteristics.

DAOISM AND THE ORIGIN OF ALL THINGS

The *Dao De Jing*, the main text of the philosophy of Daoism, views everything as the product of the interaction of two things: *wu* and *you*. *Wu* is described as "what there is not," or "the empty." *You* is the opposite: "what there is," or "the full." According to the *Dao De Jing*, *wu* and *you* are equally important. For example, a clay bowl is made up of both *you* (the clay that the potter shapes) and *wu* (the empty space it contains).

Chinese bowl

Anaximenes thought *apeiron* consisted of **air**. When this was compressed, it formed **clouds**, became **water** when even denser, and then, at its densest, **earth** and **stones**.

Firewind

According to **Heraclitus**, the fundamental principle was **fire**. This substance could become **water** and **earth**, as well as a hot and airy substance he called **"firewind."**

MATERIAL CAUSE
In Aristotle's theory, the material cause is the substance an object is made of. In ancient Greece, vases were usually made from red clay.

Clay is the material used to make the vase.

FORMAL CAUSE
This cause is the form, or shape, an object takes. In our example, the design for the vase is being worked on by an ancient Greek potter.

The form of the vase is its body with two handles.

How is the world organized?

Several philosophers have shared an interest in the structure of the world and have tried to understand the changes in it. The ancient Greeks moved away from mythological explanations, and tried to explain how the world is organized using a small number of basic principles.

In the 6th century BCE, the ancient Greek philosopher Anaximander claimed that the world and changes in it are arranged in pairs of opposites, such as wet and dry, light and dark, and hot and cold. We could even say that people's moods can be understood in this way: we are sometimes happy, and sometimes sad.

Some of this thinking was shared by Heraclitus, writing in the same century. He claimed that all things that take place in the world do so in accordance with *Logos*. This Greek term is taken to mean "rational cause," although it can also be translated as "word." The *Logos* was taken to be the "one" in which many different things were united. Like Anaximander, Heraclitus also analyzed the world in terms of opposite qualities. For him, in order to understand the world, we needed to be

A WORLD OF OPPOSITES ▶
Changing seasons can be analyzed in terms of longer, lighter, warmer, and drier days replacing shorter, darker, cooler, and wetter periods.

able to see the opposing or complex nature of things. He remarked that the ocean can be considered both pure *and* impure: to fish it is drinkable and safe; to humans it is undrinkable and dangerous.

EFFICIENT CAUSE
The creator of an object is the efficient cause. The potter takes the material to make the vase according to his design.

The potter shapes the vase on the wheel.

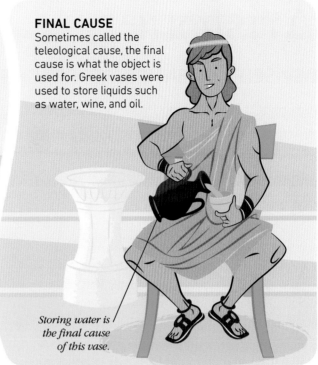

FINAL CAUSE
Sometimes called the teleological cause, the final cause is what the object is used for. Greek vases were used to store liquids such as water, wine, and oil.

Storing water is the final cause of this vase.

IT'S ALL MATH

Another 6th-century BCE Greek philosopher, Pythagoras, used a different principle to consider the world. He said that the entire Universe was organized according to harmony, and that harmony was to be found in numbers. Pythagoras was specifically referring to musical harmony. He was the first to recognize that notes played on a lyre had a mathematical relation to one another—one string produces a note, and a string that is half the length makes a note an octave higher. Pythagoras claimed to find all sorts of harmonious, mathematical relations in nature and in human life. For example, he stated that human development—stages in childhood, youth, and adulthood—could be understood in multiples of seven years.

WHAT IS A VASE?

In order to explain objects such as this Greek vase, we can think in terms of Aristotle's four "causes," which describe what the vase is made of, what shape it is, who made it, and what it's used for.

FOUR CAUSES

In the 4th century BCE, ancient Greek philosopher Aristotle tried to explain the world in terms of four "causes." If we want to know why an object is the way it is, for example, we can explain this in four ways: the material cause; the formal cause; the efficient cause; and the final cause (see above). Aristotle's point was to remind thinkers that all four factors must be kept in mind when describing the nature of things.

◄ **ANCIENT GREEK LYRE**

Pythagoras studied the workings of the harplike lyre, a popular instrument in ancient Greece. He tried to apply his understanding of musical harmony to everything in the world around him.

YIN AND YANG

Chinese philosophy considers that there are two forces within nature known as the "Yin Yang," meaning "dark-bright." Yin represents darkness, and Yang light, and these concepts are used to classify all things in the world, such as night and day, old and young, and weakness and strength. They complement rather than oppose each other, being two halves that make a whole. Yin and Yang constantly interact to enable change, but must exist in harmony, with both sides equally balanced in order to prevent chaos in the world.

Yin Yang symbol

Aristotle

DEVISED A SCIENTIFIC APPROACH TO KNOWLEDGE

Fascinated by the world around him, Aristotle developed his theories through observation, experience, and reason. A man of wide-ranging interests, he contributed to many areas of philosophy. He gave us the terms, such as ethics and metaphysics, that we still use to describe the branches of philosophy today.

Aristotle was born in 384 BCE in Stagira, Macedon, a region of northern Greece that was less developed than city-states such as Athens and Sparta. His father, Nicomachus, was well-connected, and was a doctor to the royal family at the Macedon court.

In 367 BCE Aristotle went to Athens to join the Academy—the first known university in the Western world—to study under Plato (see pp.50–51). Although he valued Plato's teachings, Aristotle went on to develop ideas that were based on very different principles from those of his mentor. Plato had claimed that everything on Earth—including concepts such as justice and virtue—was a reflection of a heaven-like world of Forms. Aristotle, however, was more like a scientist, looking at real cases and examples, trying to find features that objects and ideas had in common.

THE PRINCE'S TEACHER

A brilliant thinker, Aristotle was a natural choice to lead the Academy after Plato's death in 347 BCE, but the job was given to Plato's nephew instead. Perhaps as a result, Aristotle decided to travel, visiting Asia Minor (modern-day Turkey) and the coastal islands of Greece. However, King Philip II of Macedon soon summoned him back to tutor his son, the young prince Alexander, who grew up to become the conqueror Alexander the Great.

Aristotle returned to Athens in 335 BCE, and formed a school called the Lyceum. He wrote over 200 books in this period. One of the most famous, the *Nicomachean Ethics*, aimed to teach people how to be good. Aristotle died in 322 BCE. His writings influenced Islamic and Christian ideas in the medieval period, and many of his works survive through the translations and preserved manuscripts of Arab scholars.

Things come into **being** through **Four Causes**: material, formal, efficient, and final (see pp.20–21).

We gain **knowledge** from **experience** and **evidence** in the **world** around us (empiricism—see p.55).

The existence of **beauty** in the world represents what is **morally good**.

In **logic**, if **all humans** are animals, and **Socrates** is a **human**, then **Socrates** is an **animal** (see pp.88–89).

ARISTOTLE AND PLATO
In this famous picture, Plato (left) points upward to the heavenly world of Forms, while his pupil Aristotle reaches out into the real world, showing the difference between their philosophies.

In all things of **nature** there is something of the **marvelous**.

What is real?

When we ask a question about what is real we can mean different things. We might be asking how to distinguish between things that are real and things that are an illusion or fakes. This is dealt with in the chapter on Knowledge—see pp.42–65). Or we might be asking something more fundamental about the reality of the world itself: whether it consists of physical substance, or whether it is all in the mind.

JARGON BUSTER

Perceive To use one or more of the five senses to gain awareness of things.

Empirical Based on what is experienced, as opposed to what can be worked out by reasoning.

Philosophers who examined the nature of the world took one of two opposing views. The first view, which has a long history stretching back well over two thousand years, argues that the world is comprised of physical substance—what we call matter—and nothing else. This is known as materialism. By contrast, the second view, idealism, claims that the only reality is the world of ideas—what is in our minds.

IT'S ALL MATTER

According to the 6th-century BCE Charvaka school of thought in India, there is nothing in the world other than matter—no soul or spirit, and no god. Since we can't perceive spiritual things, this philosophy claimed that we must, at the very least, doubt them. In taking this view, Charvaka thought rejected the core beliefs of Hinduism, such as karma and reincarnation.

In the 3rd century BCE, the Greek philosopher Epicurus developed the atomic theory of Democritus (see p.19). Like Democritus, Epicurus claimed the only things that exist are "atoms" (tiny particles that make up physical bodies) and "void" (empty space). In a similar way to the materialist Charvaka school, Epicurus was led by the evidence of the senses.

Wang Chong, a Chinese thinker in the 1st century CE, also developed a materialist philosophy, in which he argued against the existence of the supernatural and ghosts. At that time, almost everyone in China believed

> # Wang stated that if **ghosts** exist, they should **appear naked**, as clothes cannot have souls.

that ghosts embodied the souls of the dead. Wang stated, somewhat humorously, that if ghosts exist, they should appear naked, as clothes cannot have souls. He also argued that if humans have ghosts, why shouldn't animals have them, too?

THE MECHANICAL UNIVERSE

The 17th-century English philosopher Thomas Hobbes and the 18th-century French thinker Julien Offray de La Mettrie both rejected the dualist philosophy of the French philosopher René Descartes, who claimed that there is an immaterial mind in addition to the material world (see p.71). According to their views, everything that exists is physical: the Universe behaves like a machine according to natural laws, and this applies to people and minds, too.

La Mettrie argued that people are no more than machines, albeit ones with feelings. Our emotions are like the "springs and gears" of a living machine that we call a human being.

IT'S ALL IN THE MIND

The 18th-century Irish philosopher and bishop George Berkeley had a completely different way of thinking from the materialists. Philosophers in this period were interested in the relationship between what is observed and our observations of them—how can we be sure that the world is actually as we perceive it to be? We can never get outside of ourselves to test the truth of our observations—we can't pass through the "veil of

Humans are like machines, just like the rest of the world.

THE UNIVERSE AS A MACHINE
According to Thomas Hobbes and Julien Offray de La Mettrie, the Universe works like a machine. Every part of it has a role to play, just as if it were a cog.

Each part works together, like a set of cogs.

25

perception" (see pp.60–61). This means we can never be sure that our perceptions really reflect the world as it is.

Berkeley, however, realized that we don't have to be concerned with "the-world-as-it-seems-to-be" at all. Perhaps reality is made up of minds and ideas—there simply are no material objects. For example, a table is merely a bundle of ideas relating to its properties: woody, squarish, hard, and smooth to the touch. He put this in Latin: *esse est percipe* ("to be is to be perceived"). All the qualities an object has are sensory ones—things that can be seen, felt, heard, and so on.

This position highlights the issue of whether objects exist if no one perceives them. For example, is the table still a table when we turn our backs on it? Idealism creates another problem, just as interesting.

If "objects" are just bundles of ideas, what is it that ties the bundle together? In the theory of idealism, there is no underlying reality to bind different ideas. So why don't these ideas drift off to attach themselves to other bundles? In Berkeley's view, the bundle stays together and the table continues to exist even when it's not being seen or touched by a person because it is constantly perceived by the mind of God.

▲ JOHNSON'S "PROOF"

Samuel Johnson famously tried to dismiss Berkeley's theory of idealism by kicking a stone to show that it was a solid object. However, he could give no actual proof that the sensation he felt was not itself an idea in the mind.

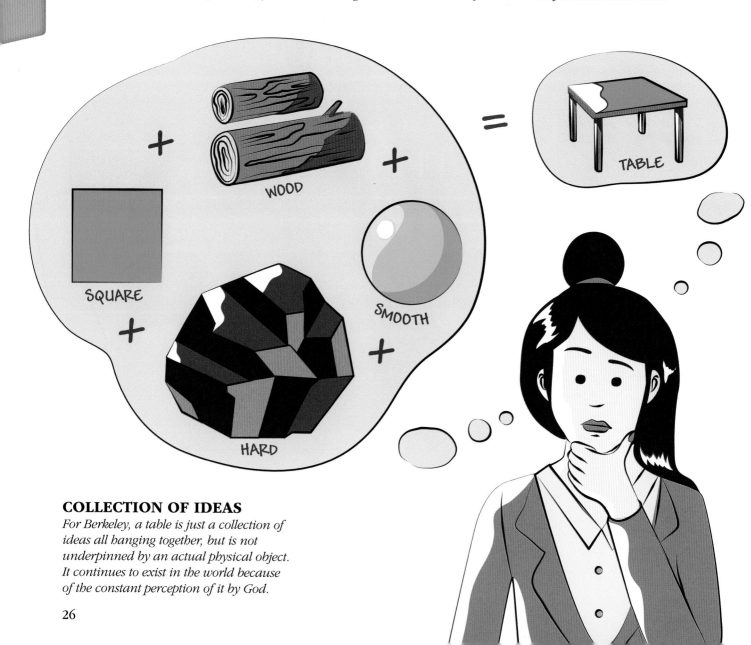

COLLECTION OF IDEAS

For Berkeley, a table is just a collection of ideas all hanging together, but is not underpinned by an actual physical object. It continues to exist in the world because of the constant perception of it by God.

SAMUEL JOHNSON'S RESPONSE

A contemporary of Berkeley's, the English writer Samuel Johnson, wanted to prove Berkeley's theory was wrong. He kicked a large stone to demonstrate the solidity of the object and the sensation it caused, saying "I refute it thus." His claim was that a mere collection of ideas would not resist his foot in the way the stone did. Johnson, however, missed the point: an idea of solidity could certainly produce another idea—that of pain.

HEGEL AND THE *GEIST*

A different form of idealism can be found in the work of the 19th-century German philosopher G.W.F. Hegel. He felt that ideas have a social context: our own ideas are shaped by those of others through shared language and beliefs. There is a kind of "collective consciousness," a single reality that he calls *Geist* ("Spirit"), which is constantly evolving.

Hegel believed that this collective consciousness, or *Geist*, evolved according to a particular process. This process starts with an initial idea (a thesis). This is widespread and accepted, but its flaws slowly generate its opposite (the antithesis). The collision of thesis and antithesis produces a new, more sophisticated idea (a synthesis), which contains essential elements of the two preceding ideas. In turn, the synthesis itself becomes a new thesis, and the process begins again. The rolling process of thesis-antithesis-synthesis in Hegel's philosophy is known as the "dialectic."

Hegel saw historical periods as a process of conflicting ideas coming together and creating new ones, and described the French Revolution in these terms. King Louis XVI refused to give the common people power. Here, the monarchy represents the thesis. The people overthrew him and established a democracy (the antithesis). When this weakened, Napoleon Bonaparte crowned himself emperor, and established new laws (the synthesis).

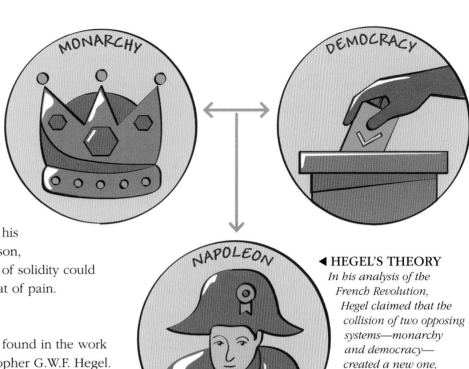

◄ **HEGEL'S THEORY**
In his analysis of the French Revolution, Hegel claimed that the collision of two opposing systems—monarchy and democracy—created a new one, the rule of Napoleon.

New laws give stability.

THE END OF METAPHYSICS?

In the 1900s, some philosophers asked whether the question of what is real was even worth asking. The English philosopher A.J. Ayer argued that if there are no empirical ways of testing hypotheses like "reality is all in the mind" or "reality is only physical," then we should give up on the question altogether.

Perhaps **reality** is made up of minds and **ideas**...

GEORG WILHELM FRIEDRICH HEGEL

G.W.F. Hegel (1775–1831) was born in what is now Germany. He had many different jobs: a private tutor, a newspaper editor, a principle, and finally a professor of philosophy. In a lot of his work, Hegel tried to make sense of the French Revolution, an event he was deeply affected by. His analysis influenced the political theories of Karl Marx very strongly. By the time of his death, Hegel was the leading philosopher in Germany.

> "All things combine together because of the properties they contain."

◀ CHARVAKA SCHOOL (6TH CENTURY BCE)
Charvaka was an ancient Indian school that rejected traditional Hindu beliefs in an eternal soul, and supernatural beings, in favor of materialism.

The idea that everything is made of matter (physical substances) is called materialism. According to this theory, even our minds and consciousness are the result of material interactions in our body. In philosophical terms, matter is the fundamental principle in the Universe.

> "Never must you come to think that Nothingness can be."

▲ PARMENIDES (c.515–c.450 BCE)
Ancient Greek Parmenides is often called the "Founder of Metaphysics" because he was the first Western thinker to consider the nature of existence.

MATERIALISM
versus
IDEALISM

In contrast to materialism, idealism argues that reality consists of minds and their ideas—things that are immaterial. This theory was held by only a few philosophers, largely in the 18th and 19th centuries.

> "Humanity is the mind of all things; the mind is the master of all things."

▲ WANG YANGMING (1472–1529)
Influential in East Asia for centuries, Chinese thinker Wang Yangming claimed that everything is connected as one: the mind and all that exists.

CITTAMĀTRA SCHOOL (4TH CENTURY CE) ▶
Also known as Yogācāra Buddhism, the Cittamātra school of thought, which began in India, claims that nothing in the Universe can exist independently of consciousness, and the observing mind.

> "The whole Universe is a mental Universe. It is similar to a dream, a mirage, a magical illusion…"

▼ DEMOCRITUS (c.460–c.370 BCE)
Ancient Greek Democritus developed the first ideas about atoms, describing them as particles that could not be divided or destroyed, and between them was empty space.

"What is the Heart, but a Spring; and the Nerves, but so many Strings; and the Joints, but so many Wheels, giving motion to the whole Body."

◄ THOMAS HOBBES (1588–1679)
According to English philosopher Hobbes, everything could be explained in terms of the machinelike interactions of material things—even the human body.

"**Nothing exists except atoms and empty space; everything else is opinion.**"

▼ BARON D'HOLBACH (1723–1789)
French-German philosopher d'Holbach rejected the idea of an all-controlling God, claiming that the world operated according to the natural laws of cause and effect.

"The Universe… presents only matter and motion… an uninterrupted succession of causes and effects."

GOTTFRIED LEIBNIZ (1646–1716) ►
For German thinker Leibniz, objects in the world are illusions, made up of what he called "monads"— unique, conscious, soul-like elements.

"All things are full of life and consciousness…"

▼ JOSIAH ROYCE (1855–1916)
The founder of American idealism, Josiah Royce held the view that all reality (including all possible truths and errors) is unified in the thought of a single, infinite consciousness—the "Absolute Knower."

"… no substance without a mind."

"Thought it is, and all things are for Thought, and in it we live and move."

▲ GEORGE BERKELEY (1685–1753)
Irish philosopher Berkeley proposed a theory of "immaterialism"—no material world; his view was that everything was either a mind or depended on a mind for its existence.

What are space and time?

Although they are quite different, space and time have one thing in common: they are the realms in which everything happens. Philosophers have asked whether space and time are real, and able to exist independently of the objects and events in them. Along with scientists, philosophers have also analyzed the relationship between time and change.

Long before scientific discoveries, philosophers used the concepts of space and time to make sense of the Universe. One of the first to question the relationship between change and time was ancient Greek philosopher Aristotle in the 4th century BCE. He regarded time as a measure of change. In fact, he thought that time is *dependent* on change—how can we tell if any time has passed if everything has stayed the same? Aristotle's theory is supported by the fact that we use two specific and regular changes to create units of time: the different positions of the Sun in the sky throughout the day, and the changing seasons over the period of a year.

Ancient Greek ideas dominated science in the West for almost 2,000 years until the 1500s and the start of the Scientific Revolution.

ARE SPACE AND TIME REAL?

Space is often thought about in terms of the objects it contains, and time is considered according to the events that happen within it. We need these concepts to make sense of a statement such as "I'm going to school tomorrow." But are space and time "real"—do they exist *independently* of these objects and events?

Two replies to this question come from a famous 18th-century rivalry between two great thinkers: the English scientist Isaac Newton and the German philosopher Gottfried Leibniz. Newton thought that space and time exist separately from the things within them—they are *substances* and do not need someone to observe them. For example, if all the stars and planets were removed, space itself would still be present, and time would tick on as regularly as before.

Leibniz took a very different view, and debated it in a series of letters to Newton's colleague, Samuel Clarke. Leibniz believed that space and time are just *relations* between objects and events. Space is simply expressed as a group of relationships between, say, Earth and the Sun. Time is expressed, for example, as the time it takes for Earth to pass a point on its orbit, and return to the same point later. Take away these relationships and the concepts of space and time would not exist.

GOTTFRIED LEIBNIZ

German philosopher Gottfried Leibniz (1646–1716) studied the works of thinkers such as Galileo, Francis Bacon, and René Descartes, and was a rationalist, believing that knowledge comes from reason. He later formed his theory of the "monad," a mindlike substance from which he thought all things were made. At the same time as Isaac Newton, Leibniz developed calculus, a type of mathematics used to describe change.

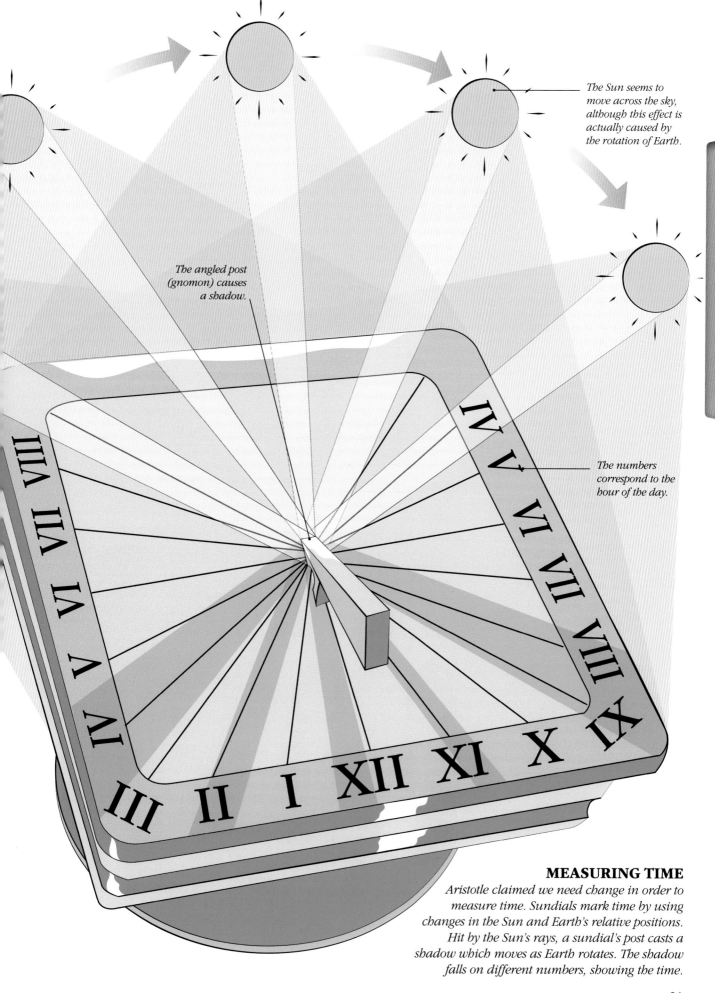

The Sun seems to move across the sky, although this effect is actually caused by the rotation of Earth.

The angled post (gnomon) causes a shadow.

The numbers correspond to the hour of the day.

MEASURING TIME

Aristotle claimed we need change in order to measure time. Sundials mark time by using changes in the Sun and Earth's relative positions. Hit by the Sun's rays, a sundial's post casts a shadow which moves as Earth rotates. The shadow falls on different numbers, showing the time.

31

◀ SOCCER GAME
Space and time are needed for us to make sense of experiences. The game of soccer wouldn't be the sport we know if the goal posts were outside the boundaries of the field, or if a goal was scored before one of these players headed it.

MAKING SENSE OF EXPERIENCES

The influential 18th-century German philosopher Immanuel Kant took a different approach from previous thinkers. In his book *Critique of Pure Reason* (1781), he asked the question: what are the conditions necessary for our experiences to make sense? One condition is that they are ordered in space and time. If events were to happen in a disorderly way, we wouldn't be able to understand anything. For example, in a soccer game, if the players were to run around randomly outside the soccer field, or if the ball were to go into the goal before the player kicked it (i.e. the effect happened before the cause), the game wouldn't make sense. As it turns out, the events in a soccer game always occur in the right place and in the right sequence—but what is it that makes them do so?

Kant's reply was this: we see events ordered in space and time because space and time are *necessary* for experiences to make sense. These concepts are like a pair of glasses that people wear (and cannot take off) that allow us to understand events. Space and time are a part of our *a priori* knowledge—things we know from reasoning (see pp.86–87).

The twins are identical in every way.

GROWING UP TOGETHER
Identical twins Li Hua and Li Juan live together. They are growing up at the same rate because they experience time from the same relative position on Earth as each other.

Li Hua

Li Juan

Li Hua

EINSTEIN'S THEORY OF RELATIVITY

Early in the 1900s, German-American scientist and mathematician Albert Einstein challenged our understanding of the nature of time and space with his theory of relativity. Einstein argued that space and time have to be considered as one thing—space-time—that varies according to the conditions. For example, time slows down for an object traveling at a very high speed, or for an object experiencing a very powerful gravitational force, such as the pull of a black hole. According to this view, space and time are definitely not *substances* (as Newton believed). They are affected by local conditions, as well as the position of the observer.

❓ SPACE TRAVEL

Einstein's theory of relativity can be explained by imagining two identical twins. One twin, Li Juan, travels in a rocket into outer space at almost the speed of light, while her sister Li Hua stays at home. When Li Juan returns, she has aged at a very different rate, as time has passed more slowly relative to her Earthbound sister.

THINK FOR YOURSELF

Imagine that you fall asleep in class. When you wake up, nothing seems to have changed. The clock shows the same time as before, and your teacher is still talking about the same subject. Yet what you don't realize is that the clock stopped while you were sleeping, and someone asked the teacher to repeat what they were saying earlier. Without change, how can you know how long you were asleep for?

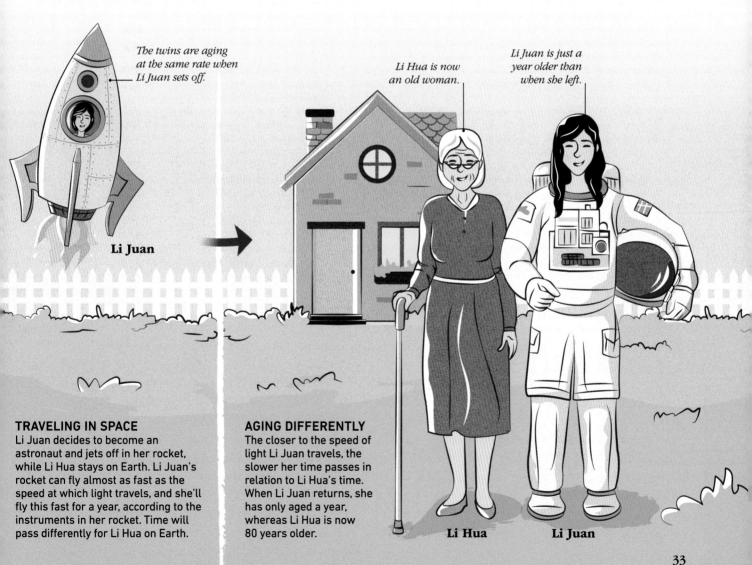

The twins are aging at the same rate when Li Juan sets off.

Li Hua is now an old woman.

Li Juan is just a year older than when she left.

Li Juan

Li Hua　　**Li Juan**

TRAVELING IN SPACE
Li Juan decides to become an astronaut and jets off in her rocket, while Li Hua stays on Earth. Li Juan's rocket can fly almost as fast as the speed at which light travels, and she'll fly this fast for a year, according to the instruments in her rocket. Time will pass differently for Li Hua on Earth.

AGING DIFFERENTLY
The closer to the speed of light Li Juan travels, the slower her time passes in relation to Li Hua's time. When Li Juan returns, she has only aged a year, whereas Li Hua is now 80 years older.

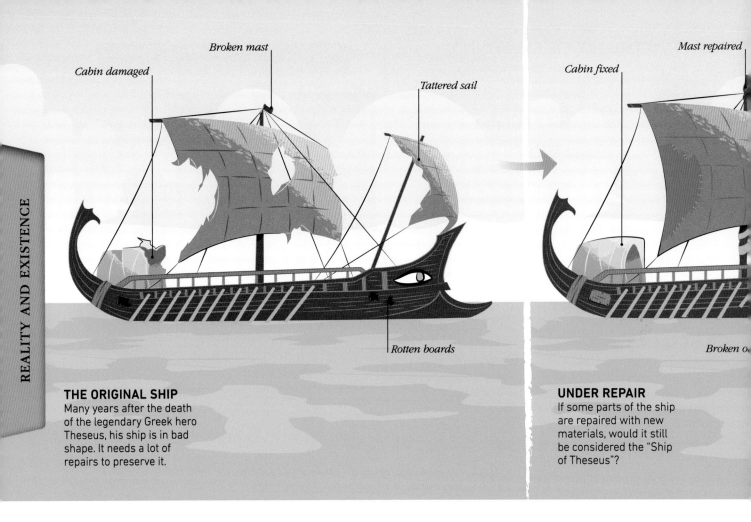

Cabin damaged

Broken mast

Tattered sail

Rotten boards

Mast repaired

Cabin fixed

Broken o

THE ORIGINAL SHIP
Many years after the death of the legendary Greek hero Theseus, his ship is in bad shape. It needs a lot of repairs to preserve it.

UNDER REPAIR
If some parts of the ship are repaired with new materials, would it still be considered the "Ship of Theseus"?

What am I?

The question of personal identity has concerned philosophers and religious thinkers from all over the world since the earliest times. They have tried to explain exactly what identifies people as individuals and whether we remain the same person throughout time, despite physical and psychological changes.

> ### JARGON BUSTER
>
> **Soul** The inner essence of something, often a human being. For some philosophers, the soul is a substance, and is believed to be immortal.
>
> **Psychology** The scientific (rather than philosophical) study of the human mind and its functions.

One answer to this question of what makes us who we are is that a human being is a thing that possesses a soul. The soul is separate from the body, is eternal (it exists forever), and remains unchanged over time. This view was shared by 4th-century BCE Greek philosopher Plato, most Christian theologians, and the 17th-century French philosopher René Descartes. There is a similar concept in Hindu philosophy, where the *atman* (meaning "breath" or "self") lies at the core of a person and defines their personality. Each of these beliefs holds that the soul, or *atman*, is only temporarily

housed in the body, and lives on after death. In some belief systems, the soul after death is said to find a new body to exist in, or moves on to a higher existence.

WHERE IS THE SOUL?
Writing in the 1700s, Scottish philosopher David Hume stated that when he examined himself for anything like a soul, he could not find it. As an empiricist, he thought that the only proof of the existence of something was to experience it, and since he claimed that it is not possible to experience a soul, it was a

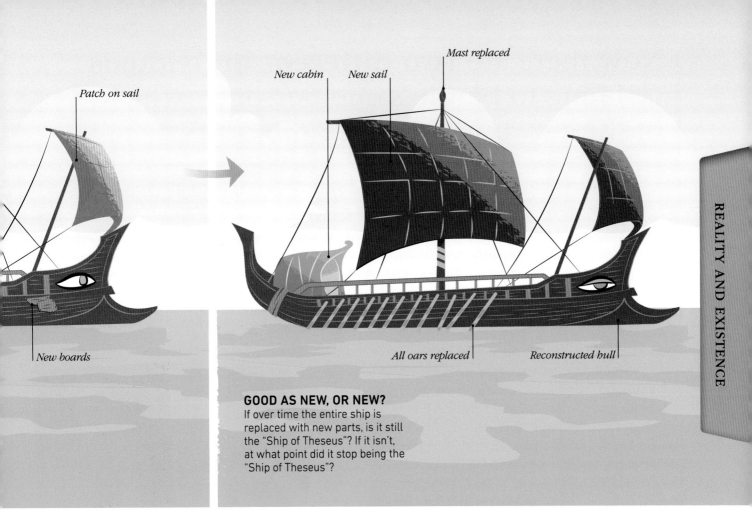

Patch on sail

New boards

New cabin   New sail   Mast replaced

All oars replaced   Reconstructed hull

GOOD AS NEW, OR NEW?
If over time the entire ship is replaced with new parts, is it still the "Ship of Theseus"? If it isn't, at what point did it stop being the "Ship of Theseus"?

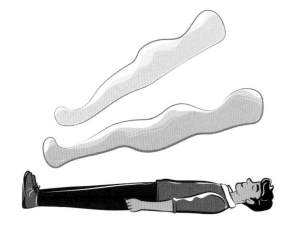

▲ **THE NATURE OF THE SOUL**
The soul is often thought of as being inside the body but not a physical part of it. Some people believe it escapes from the body after death.

mistake to think that one exists. Instead, he saw himself as being a bundle of experiences without a "center" where a soul would be.

This view is shared by Buddhists. One of the central beliefs of Buddhism is the idea that there is no unchanging, permanent self or soul at the center of a person. One of the ways Buddhists explore the changing nature of the self is through meditation.

THE SHIP OF THESEUS
The thought experiment about the physical transformation of the Ship of Theseus asks if we can still think of something as the same object if many parts of it have been removed or replaced.

CHANGING THROUGH TIME

If the soul does not exist, and therefore isn't a constant way to identify someone, what else might make a person the same today as they were yesterday? There are three possibilities: a person remains the same if they continue to have the same body; a person is unchanged if they have the same brain; a person is the same if they have the same memories and psychology.

Each of these theories faces problems. The thought experiment known as The Ship of Theseus, first recorded in the 1st century CE by ancient Greek writer Plutarch, asks questions about physical identity through time (see above). The ship sailed by a famous Greek hero called Theseus is kept in the harbor by the people of Athens in his honor. After a while, parts of the ship begin to rot, and are replaced by new ones. Eventually, after a long period of time, every piece of the ship—hull, mast, sail—has been replaced. Is it still the Ship of Theseus? In the same way, the human body changes

Now there are **two different individuals** claiming to be the same person... which of these two is the **"true"** person?

from day to day as we grow and age—our cells, blood, hair, and nails are constantly being replaced. It can't really be called the "same" body through time, can it?

TWO PEOPLE, ONE IDENTITY

Now let's examine the idea of identity being linked to the brain. A human brain has two parts: the right hemisphere and the left hemisphere. Although it remains medically impossible, it is at least conceivable that someone could have an operation in which the two hemispheres of their brain are lifted out of their body, separated, and each inserted into the empty skull of a new, brainless body (see below). Twentieth-century English philosopher Derek Parfit came up with a thought experiment to explore this idea. Suppose each hemisphere is capable of remembering past events in that person's life, and gives them the same beliefs and character. But now there are two different individuals claiming to be the same person: Lefty and Righty. Since a thing can only be identical with itself—in other words, identity is a one-to-one relation—which of these two is the "true" person?

MADE OF MEMORIES

John Locke, a 17th-century English philosopher, thought that beliefs, memories, and desires make a person who they are—what he called "psychological continuity."

Toddler   **Teenager**

However, memories can be forgotten, and beliefs, tastes, and desires can change, too. Derek Parfit challenged Locke's ideas with another thought experiment, his Teletransportation Paradox. He made a powerful argument for whether memories are the *only* elements that constitute identity (see right). Imagine a device that

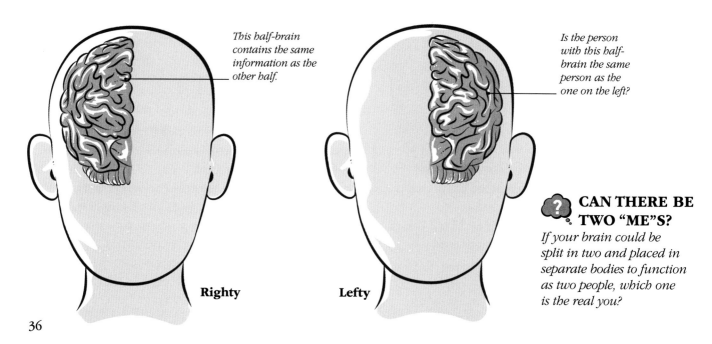

This half-brain contains the same information as the other half.

Is the person with this half-brain the same person as the one on the left?

Righty   **Lefty**

? CAN THERE BE TWO "ME"S?

If your brain could be split in two and placed in separate bodies to function as two people, which one is the real you?

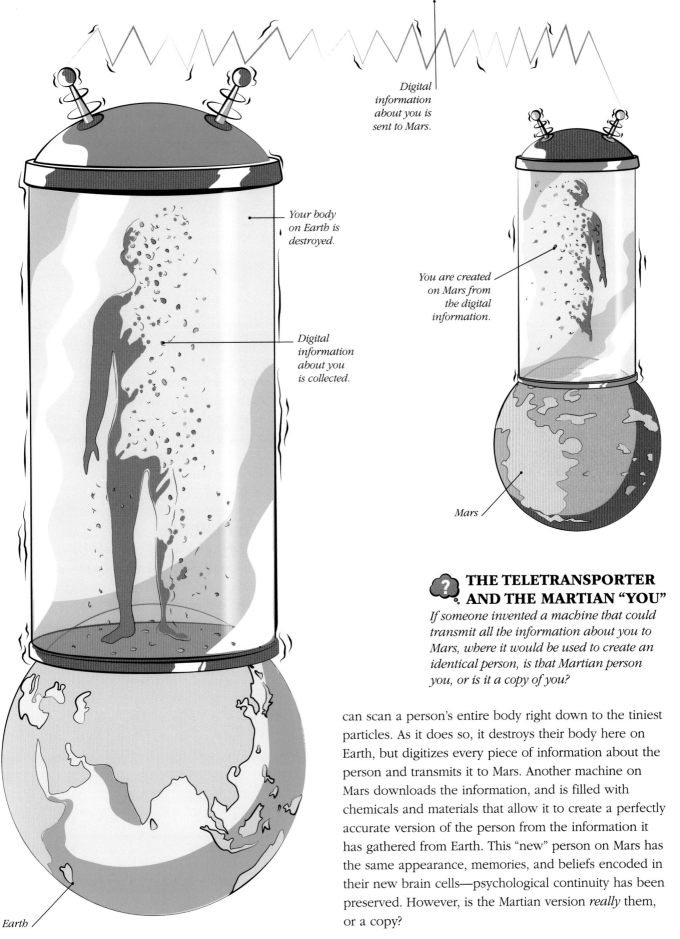

100110001110011100011011001011000011100100110001110011100

Digital information about you is sent to Mars.

Your body on Earth is destroyed.

Digital information about you is collected.

You are created on Mars from the digital information.

Mars

Earth

THE TELETRANSPORTER AND THE MARTIAN "YOU"

If someone invented a machine that could transmit all the information about you to Mars, where it would be used to create an identical person, is that Martian person you, or is it a copy of you?

can scan a person's entire body right down to the tiniest particles. As it does so, it destroys their body here on Earth, but digitizes every piece of information about the person and transmits it to Mars. Another machine on Mars downloads the information, and is filled with chemicals and materials that allow it to create a perfectly accurate version of the person from the information it has gathered from Earth. This "new" person on Mars has the same appearance, memories, and beliefs encoded in their new brain cells—psychological continuity has been preserved. However, is the Martian version *really* them, or a copy?

What is the point of my existence?

The subject of philosophy can guide people on how to live a more meaningful life. Philosophers have given many different responses to the question of why we exist. Earlier thinkers often focused on the qualities of virtue and value. More recent theories claim that the point of our existence is something that lies in our freedom to choose how we wish to live as individuals.

Many philosophers in the ancient world thought that our purpose was to try to live a "good" life (see pp.122–125). One example is Epicurus, in the 3rd century BCE, who regarded the highest good as a state of tranquility. This ultimate sense of happiness is achieved by working toward a life that is free from pain and stress. For the stoics, a rival philosophy in the same era, the state of happiness could be brought about by living a life of virtue.

This belief in the value of a virtuous life is shared by Hindu philosophy and by the ancient Greek thinker Aristotle. In Hindu philosophy, the purpose of human existence is called *purusartha*, and consists of four goals: *dharma* (morality), *artha* (wealth), *kama* (love and pleasure), and *moksha* (spiritual liberation). There is

a debate among Hindu scholars as to which of these aims is more important, and they recognize that the pursuit of wealth, and leading a spiritual life—which asks people to live in moderation—are conflicting ideas.

In the 4th century BCE, Aristotle thought that people should strive for a state of happiness by being virtuous, in keeping with good morals and our ability to reason. However, his idea of virtue is broader than simply behaving morally. It includes excelling, i.e. being the best person you can be.

NO FIXED PURPOSE

The 19th-century German philosopher Friedrich Nietzsche strongly rejected religious and moral answers to this question. In his book *Thus Spoke Zarathustra* (1885), he argued that people should find a way to transcend the pettiness of their ordinary lives, and aim for a more "heroic" version of themselves in order to flourish. The best state anyone can aspire to is something he called the *Ubermensch* ("Superman").

In the 1900s, a group of French philosophers, which included Simone de Beauvoir (see pp.40–41), Albert Camus, and Jean-Paul Sartre, focused on the nature of human existence, and developed a philosophy called

JEAN-PAUL SARTRE

Jean-Paul Sartre (1905–1980) was a French philosopher who helped to develop existentialist thinking. He believed strongly in human freedom and the importance of being true to yourself. Sartre had a lifelong relationship with feminist and fellow existentialist Simone de Beauvoir, and they often worked on ideas together. In his later years, he was dedicated to political causes, and speaking out for less privileged members of society.

There is no **fixed path** for us to follow to give **meaning** to our lives.

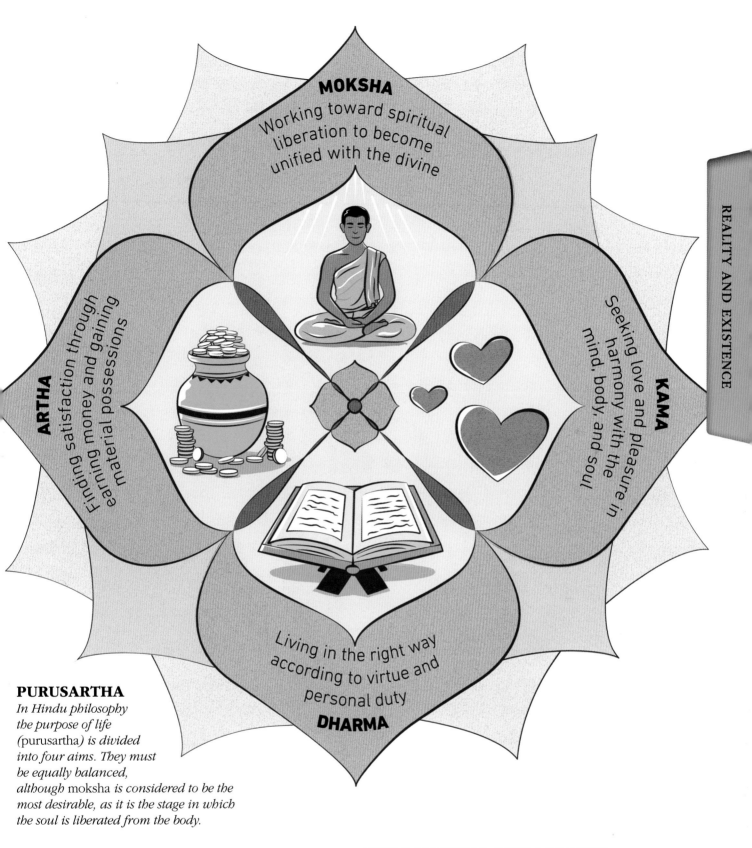

MOKSHA
Working toward spiritual liberation to become unified with the divine

KAMA
Seeking love and pleasure in harmony with the mind, body, and soul

ARTHA
Finding satisfaction through earning money and gaining material possessions

Living in the right way according to virtue and personal duty
DHARMA

PURUSARTHA
*In Hindu philosophy the purpose of life (*purusartha*) is divided into four aims. They must be equally balanced, although* moksha *is considered to be the most desirable, as it is the stage in which the soul is liberated from the body.*

existentialism (see pp.136–137). In his book *Being and Nothingness* (1943), Sartre argued, like Nietzsche, that there is no god to give us purpose, and no fixed path for us to follow to give meaning to our lives. According to Sartre, the Universe is absurd—it is chaotic and meaningless. It's therefore up to us to find a purpose for our existence, and each person's answer could be entirely different from another's.

THE LAUGHING PHILOSOPHER
The contemporary English-Italian philosopher Julian Baggini wrote a cheerful response to the gloominess of existentialism, using the British comedy group Monty Python (c.1970–c.1980) as an example. Reflecting on their comedy sketches, it becomes clear that although life can be seen as completely absurd, the best way to deal with it is by laughing at ourselves.

DEMANDING EQUAL RIGHTS
The Second Sex *set the stage for "second-wave" feminism, which involved a series of campaigns for equal rights in the 1960s, 1970s, and 1980s. Protests began in the US, such as this one in Washington, D.C., and spread throughout the world.*

I wish that every **human life** might be **pure** transparent **freedom**.

Simone de Beauvoir

FEMINIST PHILOSOPHER AND NOVELIST

A passionate activist and existential philosopher, Simone de Beauvoir dedicated much of her life to exploring the human struggle for personal freedom and equality in society. Her analysis of gender roles in particular inspired the women's liberation movement in the 20th century.

Born in Paris, France in 1908 into a bourgeois (middle-class) Catholic family, Simone de Beauvoir studied at the Sorbonne University in Paris. At the age of 21, she became the youngest person ever to pass the prestigious French exam, the *agrégation*, in philosophy. She was ranked second in her year to fellow philosopher Jean-Paul Sartre (see p.38). The pair had a relationship that lasted 50 years, although they never married, which was regarded as unconventional at the time.

De Beauvoir was profoundly affected by her experience of the Nazi occupation of Paris during World War II, and was inspired to write about the importance of standing against evil in the world, and of the pursuit of individual freedom. Her first essay, *Pyrrhus and Cineas* (1944), and the journal she founded with Sartre, *Les Temps Modernes* (1945), outlined that an individual's ability to choose freely makes them responsible for their actions—one of the central principles of existentialism.

REVOLUTIONARY IDEAS

In her most influential work, *The Second Sex* (1949), de Beauvoir analyzed how women had been treated throughout history. She argued that a person is not born into their gender, but rather grows into it, developing thoughts and behaviors that conform to society's expectations. Her views inspired women around the world to speak up against oppression.

De Beauvoir always considered herself to be an author and activist rather than a philosopher. In fact, during her lifetime many of her own philosophical ideas were considered to be those of Sartre. It was not until after her death in 1986 that she gained the recognition she deserved as an independent thinker. Her lasting contributions to politics, ethics, feminism, and existentialism have made her a remarkable figure in Western philosophy.

Existentialism states that people are **free** to make **choices**, whether moral or immoral, and that they must accept the **consequences** (see pp.136–137).

The idea of **femininity** was created by and for men; **women are free** to define themselves (see pp.178–179).

Our **pursuit of freedom** should not limit someone else's ability to do the same.

"Bad faith" is refusing to live an **"authentic"** life, **accepting a role** given by society, and not standing up for your own beliefs.

KNOWLEDGE

The study of knowledge is called epistemology. It analyzes what knowledge is, how we gain it, and whether there is anything that we just can't know. The debate about what kinds of belief count as knowledge began in ancient times. Since then, philosophers have continued to question the nature of knowledge and the limits of what we can know.

What can we know?

Many of the earliest Greek philosophers were interested in knowing how the world around them worked. But soon philosophers also started to question the characteristics of this knowledge itself. These early thinkers began a whole new area within philosophy, and one of the first questions they asked was about what it is possible for us to know.

The ancient Greek Xenophanes, who lived in the 6th to 5th centuries BCE, was the earliest Western philosopher whose thoughts about human knowledge have survived. He made the distinction between knowing something, and believing something. Suppose you believe that there are an even number of stars in the galaxy. This might possibly be true, but just because you

THE SOCRATIC METHOD

Socrates used question and answer conversations to explore concepts such as truth and justice. This technique is now known as the Socratic Method. Philosophers can use it to explore even simple sounding problems—for example, what makes a chair a chair?

Excuse me, I'd like to **BUY A CHAIR**.

Of course, but **WHAT DO YOU MEAN BY A CHAIR?**

What do I mean? I mean **A PIECE OF FURNITURE THAT HAS FOUR LEGS**, of course.

I see. So **WOULD YOU BE INTERESTED IN ITEM 1?** It has four legs.

What? No, of course I don't want that. **I WANT SOMETHING FOR SITTING ON**.

My apologies. So I suppose you **WOULDN'T BE INTERESTED IN ITEM 2 THEN?**

I MIGHT BE! Why wouldn't I?

Well, it **DOESN'T HAVE FOUR LEGS...**

An **unexamined life** is **not** worth **living**.

SOCRATES, 5th century BCE

believe it, does it mean you know it's true? This raises a problem which has come up again and again throughout the history of philosophy—how can we be sure about what it's possible for us to know? Xenophanes' doubts about knowledge make him a skeptic—someone who questions whether we can properly know things.

DOUBTING EVERYTHING

The 5th-century BCE Greek philosopher Socrates was also skeptical about whether we could have knowledge. He once even famously said that he couldn't really claim to know anything at all. Socrates appears as a character in many works written by his student, Plato. Here he is shown using a particular method to question what people thought they knew. Plato presented this method as a dialogue (conversation) in which Socrates asked a series of questions about a topic—for example, the nature of justice. The aim was to identify the flaws in people's beliefs about what they thought they knew.

THE EVIL DEMON

More than two thousand years after Socrates, the 17th-century French philosopher René Descartes questioned the knowledge that we appear to gain through our

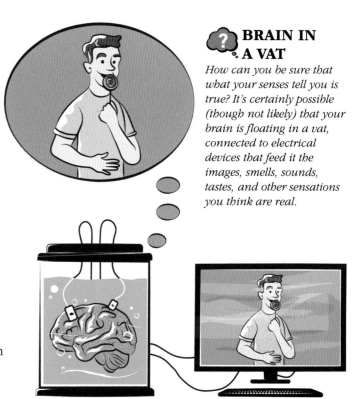

KNOWLEDGE

BRAIN IN A VAT

How can you be sure that what your senses tell you is true? It's certainly possible (though not likely) that your brain is floating in a vat, connected to electrical devices that feed it the images, smells, sounds, tastes, and other sensations you think are real.

senses. Do these senses ever let us down? If so, what reason do we have to trust them? Descartes suggested the possibility that an evil demon with extraordinary powers is deceiving us. This demon might be fooling our senses to hide the world as it really is. If this is true, we can't be sure of anything we think we know.

Descartes, Socrates, and other skeptics raised serious questions about what it's possible for us to know—and many philosophers have dedicated themselves to answering these questions ever since.

SOCRATES

Socrates (c.470–399 BCE) was an influential philosopher who lived in Athens, Greece. Although he left no written works of his own, we know about his ideas through his student Plato. Socrates challenged the views of others, and worked toward clearly defining concepts such as beauty and honor through debate. Unpopular with the Athenian authorities, he was sentenced to death for not believing in the gods and for "corrupting" the youth of Athens.

SKEPTICISM

Skepticism is a philosophical viewpoint that questions whether we can ever know anything for sure. Skeptics through the ages have either denied any possibility of knowledge, or have taken the view that the existence of knowledge cannot be proved or disproved either way.

"Those that claim knowledge cannot be stating actual facts."

◄ AJÑANA SCHOOL (6TH CENTURY BCE)
Followers of this ancient Indian philosophy believed that it was impossible to gain knowledge by discussing philosophical theories.

▼ XENOPHANES (C.570–C.475 BCE)
The ancient Greek poet and philosopher Xenophanes criticized people who tried to describe the gods. This fragment of his poetry appears to warn against claiming to have knowledge about the unknown.

"The clear and certain truth no human has seen."

"He didn't know if he was Zhuangzi who had dreamt he was a butterfly, or a butterfly dreaming that he was Zhuangzi."

ZHUANGZI ▲ (C.369–C.286 BCE)
In his story "The Butterfly Dream," Chinese philosopher Zhuangzi accepts his inability to truly know what is real from what is not.

◄ SOCRATES (C.470–C.399 BCE)
The ancient Greek philosopher Socrates famously claimed that he didn't really know anything for certain.

"All I know is that I know nothing."

"The human understanding is of its own nature prone to suppose the existence of more order and regularity in the world than it finds."

▲ FRANCIS BACON (1561–1626)
The English philosopher Bacon highlighted the importance of questioning our assumptions, which might be mistaken, before using them as the basis of scientific conclusions.

▼ RENÉ DESCARTES (1596–1650)
The French philosopher Descartes used his "method of doubt" to analyze his beliefs to see whether any of them could really be proved.

"In order to seek truth, it is necessary once in the course of our life, to doubt, as far as possible, of all things."

"Doubt is not a pleasant condition, but certainty is absurd."

▲ VOLTAIRE (1694–1778)
The French thinker Voltaire warned against forming beliefs and preaching them to others without first making sure to rigorously question and test them.

▼ DAVID HUME (1711–1776)
According to the Scottish philosopher David Hume, our knowledge of what has happened in the past cannot be a guide for what will happen in the future.

"The past may be no rule for the future."

"I think I have the courage to doubt everything… But I do not have the courage to know anything."

▲ SØREN KIERKEGAARD (1813–1855)
Danish thinker Kierkegaard urged people to be brave enough to discover their own personal truths by doubting traditional beliefs.

"Those who do not doubt do not believe."

◄ MIGUEL DE UNAMUNO (1864–1936)
The Spanish philosopher Unamuno said that beliefs can only be maintained by resolving the doubts we have about them.

47

What is knowledge?

Philosophers have always asked about the nature of knowledge. In ancient Greece, the 4th-century BCE thinker Plato suggested that beliefs must be true and justified to count as knowledge. This was accepted without much disagreement by Western philosophers until the late 1900s, when the definition of knowledge was seriously questioned.

To know something is to hold some kind of belief. This belief should be reasonably strong—if you aren't quite sure of a fact, you couldn't say that you know it. If you guess during a quiz you can't say that you "know" the answer, even if it turns out to be correct. For belief to count as knowledge, it must also be true. You can't "know" something if it isn't really true. In addition, the belief must be justified—meaning that there must be good evidence for holding the belief in the first place. Some kinds of evidence may be better than others. Most people would trust the evidence of their senses, but this isn't always enough. If you saw somebody dressed up as a vampire at a party, you wouldn't be justified in believing in vampires.

Appearances   **Reality**

◄ MOVIE SET
A person in the middle of a street on a movie set would be justified in believing that they were looking at whole buildings, but this wouldn't be true, so this belief doesn't count as knowledge.

THINK FOR YOURSELF

Imagine you see your friend Joshua in a shoe store, and therefore believe you "know" that Joshua is in the store. It turns out that who you really saw is Joshua's identical twin brother, James. However, Joshua actually is in the store—he's just bent down out of sight. So while it's true that your friend Joshua is in the store, do you think it's right to say you "knew" this?

QUESTIONING KNOWLEDGE

A few philosophers throughout history tried to show that this definition of knowledge as justified true belief doesn't really work. But it became a very popular explanation of knowledge in 17th-century Europe, and continued to be generally accepted for the next few centuries. The definition wasn't widely questioned until 1963, when an American philosopher named Edmund Gettier argued that some beliefs are both true and are justified by good evidence, but don't really seem like they should count as knowledge. Gettier said that while it is necessary for beliefs to be both true and justified to be considered knowledge, that's not always sufficient (enough). Something further is required.

GETTIER CASES

Examples that illustrate Gettier's point have come to be known as Gettier cases or Gettier problems. For instance, suppose you pass a clocktower at 5:23 pm, and you look up and see the time it is showing. The hour hand of the clock happens to be pointing to 5, while the minute hand is pointing to 23. You form the belief that it is 5:23 pm. However, what you don't know is that the clock stopped this morning at exactly 5:23 am. You just happened to pass it at the correct time.

The three conditions for knowledge seem to be satisfied. You have a strong belief that it is 5:23 pm, and it is true that it is 5:23 pm. And you have the evidence

BELIEF

If the girl says "that's my cat" she must **BELIEVE** that it's her cat, or she cannot possibly know that it is.

If the cat were covered in soot, the girl may **BELIEVE** "that's my cat" and it may be **TRUE**, but she has **NO EVIDENCE** for her belief.

TRUTH

The girl's statement "that's my cat" must actually be **TRUE** to count as knowledge.

KNOWLEDGE

A statement must be at least **BELIEVED**, **JUSTIFIED**, and **TRUE** to count as **KNOWLEDGE**.

If two cats look very similar, there may be good **EVIDENCE** for the girl to **BELIEVE** "that's my cat" even when it is **NOT TRUE**.

If the girl mistakenly thinks her cat is at home, she does **NOT BELIEVE** "that's my cat," despite there being good **EVIDENCE** in front of her that it is true.

The girl's belief of "that's my cat" must be **JUSTIFIED** by the evidence.

JUSTIFICATION

THAT'S MY CAT!

THAT'S MY CAT!

Phrases like "that's my cat" are statements of belief about how things are in the world. These beliefs might count as knowledge if they meet certain minimum requirements.

of your own eyes to justify your belief. But is this really knowledge? You are only accidentally right. So—what other condition needs to be added to our list? And what if there are ways around that, too? Since Gettier first pointed out the problems with the accepted definition of knowledge, philosophers have tried to find a new one. As yet, no one has come up with an alternative that is widely accepted. While we can still talk about "knowing" things, it turns out that it's trickier to say what we mean by "knowledge" than it may at first appear.

PLATO AND HIS STUDENTS
Much like students at a modern university, the scholars at Plato's Academy were taught to think for themselves, rather than just follow the views of their teacher. The most famous of Plato's students at the Academy was Aristotle (see pp.22–23).

Until **philosophers** are **kings... cities** will never have **rest** from their **evils**.

Plato

FOUNDER OF WESTERN PHILOSOPHY

The ancient Greek thinker Plato is the first Western philosopher whose writings have survived intact—philosophy from before Plato only exists as fragments in later philosophers' works. To this day, Plato's ideas contribute to our thinking about knowledge, ethics, the nature of the mind, and how we should organize society.

Plato was born in the Greek city-state of Athens in c.429 BCE to a rich and influential family. He was expected to enter politics, but instead joined a young group of Athenians who kept company with Socrates (see p.45). This great philosopher became Plato's mentor and idol. When Socrates was sentenced to death in 399 BCE for corrupting the minds of the youth of Athens, Plato was so outraged that he left Greece to travel. On his return to Athens in 387 BCE, a number of other scholars began to meet regularly to learn from Plato, and the group became known as the Academy.

WRITING AND TEACHING

Plato's philosophical writings take the form of dialogues (conversations), usually between Socrates and other thinkers and friends. Plato himself never featured in them. It is hard to know whether they were real debates that Socrates had, or Plato's own thoughts. A few dialogues concern the trial and execution of Socrates. The last in this series, the *Phaedo*, movingly recorded the final hours of Socrates, spent with his friends. Plato expressed dissatisfaction with Athenian politics in his most celebrated work, the *Republic*. He proposed a more stable but less democratic system, in which the people would be ruled by "philosopher-kings" who had trained in philosophy from childhood.

Plato traveled to Syracuse, Sicily in c.366 BCE to help the young Dionysus II become a wise and just ruler. However, his student proved to be a poor politician—not the philosopher-king Plato had in mind. After two years, Plato returned to teaching at the Academy in Athens, remaining there until his death in 347 BCE.

If people learn the nature of **"the good,"** they will never act badly (see p.186).

The **psyche**, or soul, is eternal and immaterial. It is divided into three parts: the logical, the spirited, and the appetitive (see p.68).

We recognize things and concepts in the real world because we have innate knowledge of the ideal **world of Forms** (see pp.52–53).

Ordinary people cannot be trusted to make good decisions, so only experts—**"philosopher-kings"**—should decide on matters of state (see p.164).

Where does knowledge come from?

Throughout the history of philosophy, there has been a long and lively debate about where knowledge comes from. Some philosophers, known as rationalists, have argued that knowledge is something that we are born with, or that we can work toward it using our reasoning alone. Rejecting this view, empiricists believe that knowledge can come only from our experience of the world.

In Western philosophy, the discussion of where knowledge comes from began in ancient Greece, where the great thinkers Plato and Aristotle argued for opposing theories about how we come to understand the world around us. This opposition arose again in the 1600s during the Age of Enlightenment, a period in which many European thinkers started to question previously established ways of thinking.

KNOWLEDGE FROM WITHIN

The 4th-century BCE ancient Greek philosopher Plato was a rationalist who claimed that knowledge is something that we are born with, and that we just need to be reminded of what we already know. He said that the soul, before it arrives in this world and inhabits the body,

The shadows are cast by statues or other **models of objects that only exist in the real world**.

The **shadows on the cave wall** represent our **imperfect knowledge** of how things really are.

Humans are compared to **prisoners** who mistake the **shadows that pass in front of them** for reality.

is already equipped with ideas from a heavenlike world of pure ideas. Plato called these ideas Forms. According to him, everything we see around us, without exception, is an imperfect version of what exists in the world of Forms. For example, when we recognize an object as a chair, this is because in some way it reminds us of the perfect idea of a chair that we already have within us.

In his *Meno* (c.385 BCE) Plato argued that all learning is a matter of recollection. The main character in the *Meno*, who is based on Plato's real-life teacher, is Socrates. He asks an uneducated, enslaved boy questions about a mathematical problem, and guides him toward the solution. Socrates claims that the boy's ability to solve the puzzle is proof that the mathematical knowledge was already within him. Socrates had only made him recall what he knew all along.

EVERYTHING IS SHADOWS

In the *Republic* (c.375 BCE), Plato presents an allegory (a story that has a hidden meaning) that illustrates his ideas about knowledge. The Allegory of the Cave compares human existence to the experience of being imprisoned in a cave for our entire lives. The only things we are able to see in this cave are shadows cast on a wall, which we mistake for reality. One prisoner, representing a philosopher, escapes their chains, and leaves the cave. On their way out, they are blinded by the light of the Sun, which represents the true source of knowledge, our reason. But emerging from the cave, the prisoner can see the world as it really is. Through this allegory, Plato argues that knowledge gained through our senses is always unreliable, and only knowledge that comes from reasoning can be trusted. We must allow ourselves to be freed by the teachings of philosophers, who have glimpsed the real world, which is the world of Forms.

THE ALLEGORY OF THE CAVE

Plato's story of the prisoners in the cave highlights the importance of trusting philosophical guidance, and of using our reason to escape from the illusions of the senses.

The **light of the Sun** represents true enlightenment, which can only be understood by **the philosopher**.

The **wall separates the prisoners** from the rest of the cave and the outside world, which is the **world of Forms**.

The **fire deceives** the prisoners into believing shadows to be reality. It stands for **artificial sources of knowledge**.

An **escaped prisoner** finds the true light of the Sun blinding; the **path to truth** can have this effect.

REASONING FROM DOUBT

More than two thousand years after Plato, the 17th-century French philosopher René Descartes also relied on a rationalist approach to knowledge. He asked: "Is there one piece of knowledge that is so obviously true that it could act as a foundation for the rest of knowledge?" He set about doubting everything, and realized that the only thing he couldn't doubt was the fact that he was doubting. He reasoned that doubting is a form of thinking, so it must be the case that he exists—there must be somebody doing this thinking. This led to his famous statement, "I think; therefore, I am."

Having established that he must have a mind to do this thinking, Descartes went on to investigate how he could come to possess a mind, which he saw as

In Eastern philosophy, knowledge is linked to our ability to act morally, rather than our abilities to reason and to experience.

something infinite and perfect. He argued that it must have been planted in him by a perfect God, like the signature on a piece of craftsmanship. For Descartes, this not only explained how he could have a mind, it was also proof that God exists. Descartes assumed that this God must be benevolent (kindly), and so would not allow humans to think the world is something other than what it seems. In this way, Descartes reasoned his way from the fact of his own existence to a proof that the external world exists, all without relying on the evidence of his senses.

I think therefore I am.

RENÉ DESCARTES, *Discourse on the Method* (1637)

LEARNING FROM EXAMPLES

The other great philosophical tradition that looks for a source for knowledge is empiricism, which argues against the idea that we are born with knowledge. Followers of empiricism claim that knowledge can only come from experiencing the world. The 4th-century BCE ancient Greek philosopher Aristotle was perhaps the first empiricist. He trusted that our senses are reliable in helping us to understand the world. In the absence of

The body that I can feel might be an illusion.

Do I have a **BODY?**

How can I trust that what my senses show me actually exists?

Is there an **OUTSIDE WORLD?**

If I were not thinking, it would be impossible to doubt that I am thinking.

Am I **THINKING?**

THINKING IS EXISTING
Descartes suggested that even if we are being deceived about the existence of the outside world or even about having a body, the one thing that we cannot doubt is that we are able to think.

✓ FOUR LEGS
✓ BARKS
✓ MAMMAL
✓ CANINE
✓ HAS FUR
✓ EATS MEAT

▲ WHAT IS "DOGGINESS"?
Aristotle said that we know we are looking at a dog by comparing what is in front of us with previous experiences of things that we have labeled "dog." Our concept of "dogginess" is a collection of qualities we use to recognize dogs in the world.

the senses, he insisted, it would be impossible to learn anything at all. He thought that knowledge of "a chair," "a dog," or "the color yellow" were acquired by studying examples of them. A dog is not a dog because it matches up to a perfect idea of a dog in a world of Forms. It's a dog because it has an essential "dogginess"—the features of a dog, which we learn through our previous experience of dogs. Therefore, we must study the world to gain knowledge.

EXPERIENCE MATTERS

The 17th-century philosopher John Locke agreed with Aristotle's empiricist view of knowledge. But he took the idea further, arguing that the mind is a *tabula rasa* (a blank slate) when we are born—we are not born with knowledge. We have to learn in order to understand, so what it is possible for us to know depends on the information that is filtered through to us from our senses. We need to taste juice, see trees, hear music, and touch surfaces in order to have a proper idea of all these things. Once we have experienced these things through our senses, we retain a copy of our perceptions in our minds, and they become concepts. We then use these concepts to recognize other examples that we find around us—so experiences are necessary in order to understand the world.

To illustrate Locke's view, imagine that you asked a person who had been visually impaired from birth about the concept of red. Because they've never seen the color, they cannot know what it looks like, and therefore cannot create a concept of it in their mind.

Locke went on to explain that objects have what he called "qualities," which have the power to produce ideas in our minds. Primary qualities are things like size and shape, which produce ideas that "resemble" these objects—our idea of the roundness of a ball matches up to the roundness of the ball that we observe. Secondary qualities produce ideas that do not relate to features that the object has in itself. For example, a blue ball looks blue because of how our senses interpret light, rather than the "blueness" being contained in the ball itself.

The debate between empiricism and rationalism reached its peak in the 17th and 18th centuries, with empiricism being championed in Britain and Ireland, while many continental European philosophers argued the case for rationalism. Near the end of the 1700s, a German philosopher named Immanuel Kant came up with a theory of knowledge that combined the two opposing viewpoints into one (see pp.60–61).

◄ A BLANK SLATE
Locke believed that we are not born with knowledge. He compared the mind at birth to a "blank slate" with nothing written on it. Only through having experiences during our lives do we start to fill in these blank spaces.

THINK FOR YOURSELF

Think of an orange: its shape, size, texture, color, and smell. Is it easy for you to form an idea of all these features in your mind, even without the orange in front of you? According to the philosophy of the 17th-century English thinker John Locke, we are able to visualize the orange clearly because we have learned its qualities from past experience. The senses help us form concepts in our minds from the objects we come into contact with.

John Locke

DEFENDER OF EMPIRICISM AND INDIVIDUAL RIGHTS

John Locke was a champion of empiricism—the view that all knowledge comes from experience. Locke argued that because we slowly build up knowledge, we cannot be certain in our beliefs. This idea influenced Locke's political writings, in which he argued that authorities should not impose their beliefs on the people.

John Locke was born in 1632 in Wrington, a village in southwest England. His parents were strict Puritans (members of a religious group that sought to reform and simplify the Church of England). His father had connections with an influential member of Parliament, so Locke received an excellent education. While studying languages and medicine at Oxford University, Locke met Anthony Ashley Cooper, the 1st Earl of Shaftesbury. He became Shaftesbury's personal doctor in 1667, and also advised him on political matters. Shaftesbury helped to inspire Locke's revolutionary ideas on the nature of individual rights and of society.

RULE BY THE PEOPLE

Locke's political views were dangerous at the time, because he supported the opponents of the monarchy. He was eventually forced to leave England in 1683, and went to live in Holland. Locke spent his time in exile writing about knowledge and politics, and working on what would later become his masterpiece, *An Essay Concerning Human Understanding* (1689). He returned to England after the bloodless revolution of 1688, in which William of Orange and his wife Mary replaced King James II. This event shifted the balance of power in England from the throne to Parliament. In his book *Two Treatises of Government* (1690), Locke famously rejected the belief that monarchs were given the right to rule by God. He argued that societies must instead form governments by mutual agreement.

Locke died in 1704, but his revolutionary theories on knowledge had a huge impact on later empiricists. In the late 1700s, his political ideas greatly influenced the foundation of democratic principles in the laws of both France and the United States.

At birth the mind is a **tabula rasa**, or **blank slate**. We fill our minds with ideas as we **experience** the world **through our senses** (see p.55).

Human beings originally existed in a **state of nature**, in which everyone was free to do as they pleased, so long as they preserved **peace** and the state of **humankind in general** (see pp.160–161).

Information is filtered through our **unreliable senses,** so we have to conclude **general laws** from **particular instances**. This leaves **room for error**.

Humans are born with natural rights to **life, liberty, and property**. The denial of these rights is against God's wishes.

THE POWER OF PARLIAMENT
In 1689 the English monarchy signed the Bill of Rights, a document that incorporated many of Locke's political ideals. It gave Parliament, seen here in the early 1700s, control of the English economy and army, and protected individual rights. It influenced the US Bill of Rights, composed almost a century later.

Being all **equal and independent**, no one ought to harm another in **life**, **health, liberty, or possessions.**

The Greek philosopher Plato said that we are born with knowledge. When we learn, we access ideas that we already have, deep inside our minds.

"What we call learning is only a process of recollection."

"From time to time I have found that the senses deceive, and it is prudent never to trust completely those who have deceived us even once."

Rationalism is the view that the mind is the chief source of knowledge. Rationalists argue that certain truths, particularly those in logic and mathematics, can be understood directly by the mind without any reference to the outside world.

▲ RENÉ DESCARTES (1596–1650)
The French thinker Descartes argued that we can't trust our senses, so the only certain knowledge that we have must come from reasoning alone.

RATIONALISM
versus
EMPIRICISM

▼ FRANCIS BACON (1561–1626)
English thinker and politician Bacon popularized the "scientific method"—an approach to gaining knowledge that is based on carefully observed facts.

Empiricism rejects the idea that knowledge comes from within. The source of knowledge is experience of the world around us. Empiricism was a hugely influential idea in Britain in the 17th and 18th centuries.

"By far the best proof is experience."

ARISTOTLE ▶
(384–322 BCE)
Though the Greek philosopher Aristotle had rationalist ideas, he also claimed that knowledge is gained empirically. To know what something is, we compare what we see in the world around us to our previous experiences.

"Truth resides in the world around us."

The Jewish-Dutch philosopher Spinoza said that because our sense organs have physical limitations, the experiences they produce in our minds can be faulty.

"There are truths of reasoning and truths of fact."

"The fictitious, the false, do not arise from the very power of the mind, but from external causes."

▲ GOTTFRIED LEIBNIZ (1646–1716)
According to the German thinker Leibniz, the human mind can only grasp a small number of truths by reasoning alone. We must also rely on experience to give us "truths of fact."

NICOLAS MALEBRANCHE ▶
(1638–1715)
A deeply religious French philosopher, Malebranche said that the ideas we have in our minds are divine, because they are given to us by God.

"Faith must regulate our mind's path; but it is only sovereign reason which fills it with understanding."

JOHN LOCKE ▶
(1632–1704)
The English philosopher Locke believed that the mind is a "blank slate" at birth. All knowledge comes exclusively through experience.

"No man's knowledge can go beyond his experience."

▼ DAVID HUME (1711–1776)
Scottish philosopher Hume challenged the idea that we are born with knowledge, arguing that it can only come from experience of the world.

"We cannot form to ourselves a just idea of the taste of a pineapple, without having actually tasted it."

"The perception of distance by the eye [is] an inference… we learn to make; and which we make with more and more correctness as our experience increases."

▲ JOHN STUART MILL (1806–1873)
For the English philosopher Mill, even mathematical principles are formed from generalizations that we make based on our experiences.

Are there limits to knowledge?

If what we can know is limited only by what there is to know, then we could go on discovering more about the Universe until there is nothing left to find out. In the 1700s, the German philosopher Immanuel Kant (see pp.62–63) suggested that there are further limitations to knowledge, and that there are some things that we may never be able to know for certain.

(see pp.62–63)

JARGON BUSTER

Empiricism The view that all knowledge of things that exist outside the mind is acquired through the experiences of the senses.

Innate A quality or a feature that a person is born with naturally.

Rationalism The view that we can gain knowledge of the world through the use of reasoning, without relying on the experiences of our senses.

Kant was heavily influenced by the work of David Hume, an 18th-century Scottish philosopher. Hume was an empiricist (see pp.58–59) who argued that everything we know comes from the experiences of our senses. He said that if knowledge can only come from the senses, then it is impossible to see the cause of an event. He used the example of a game of billiards, which is similar to pool or snooker. A cue strikes a ball, which then moves across a table. The cue seems to cause the movement of the ball, but if we look closely, do we see the cause? We only really see two events that happen together—the cue hitting the ball, and the ball moving. We don't experience the cause of the ball's movement, so for Hume it is something we cannot know.

▲ REPRESENTING THE WORLD
Kant likened the way we perceive things to the way a painter presents an image. A painting can portray all the details of a scene, but it's just a representation, it's not the scene itself.

THE WORLD IN ITSELF

Kant built on Hume's points. He argued that what we experience must always be interpreted through our bodies—our senses, brains, and central nervous systems. Our bodies create representations in our minds of the world around us. Kant called the world as we perceive it through these representations the "phenomenal" world. But it is impossible for us to get

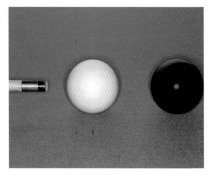

◄ CAUSE AND EFFECT
According to Hume, although we can see a cue hit a ball on a pool table, we have no way to be able to "see" that this is the cause of the ball's movement.

outside of our bodies to find out if the representations that we perceive match what Kant called the "noumenal" world—the world as it actually is in itself. This world is forever hidden to us behind what Kant called the "veil of perception."

Though Kant said the world as it is in itself is beyond our reach, he did believe that it exists. He claimed that for us to have experiences of things that exist in the noumenal world, there must be things actually existing in that world. Kant argued that we can at least have knowledge that this noumenal world actually does exist, even if we can say nothing more about it.

On the other hand, things that we cannot experience directly at all can never be a part of the phenomenal world, and therefore are things that we will never know anything about. For Kant, the existence and nature of God—which we cannot directly experience—must be left as matters of faith.

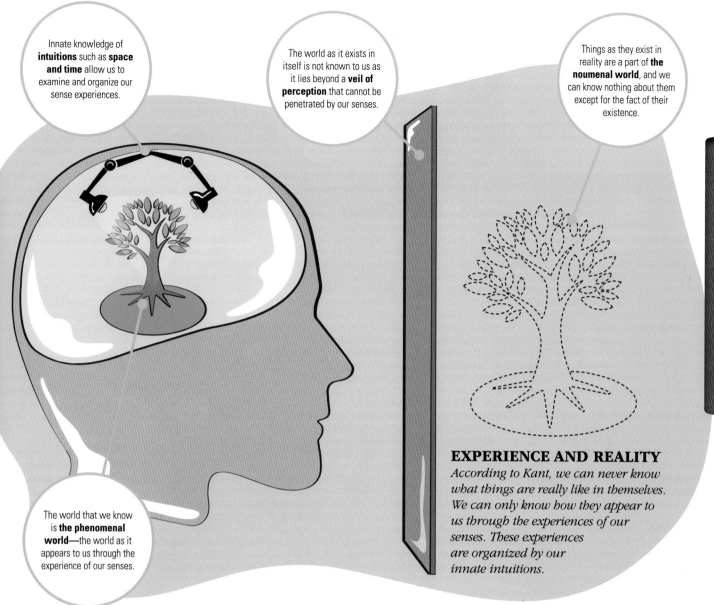

Innate knowledge of **intuitions** such as **space and time** allow us to examine and organize our sense experiences.

The world as it exists in itself is not known to us as it lies beyond a **veil of perception** that cannot be penetrated by our senses.

Things as they exist in reality are a part of **the noumenal world**, and we can know nothing about them except for the fact of their existence.

The world that we know is **the phenomenal world**—the world as it appears to us through the experience of our senses.

EXPERIENCE AND REALITY

According to Kant, we can never know what things are really like in themselves. We can only know how they appear to us through the experiences of our senses. These experiences are organized by our innate intuitions.

INNATE INTUITIONS

Kant is often said to have created a unified theory of knowledge that combined the traditions of rationalism and empiricism (see pp.52–55 and 58–59). This is because, unlike Hume, Kant didn't believe that knowledge comes from the senses alone. He believed, like the rationalists, that some things are known by us innately from birth. For instance, we don't "learn" from our experiences that time is passing, or that objects exist in three dimensions. So our ideas of time and space must be innate (see p.32). Kant believed that these innate ideas, which he called intuitions, help us to make sense of our experiences.

REPRESENTATION AND WILL

A great admirer of Kant, the 19th-century German philosopher Arthur Schopenhauer was also influenced by reading Eastern philosophy. He saw Kant's

phenomenal and noumenal worlds as similar to the distinction between *atman* (soul—see p.34) and *brahman* (reality) in Hindu philosophy. What Kant called the phenomenal world, Schopenhauer labeled the world of Representation. But he argued that we have special knowledge of one thing in the external or noumenal world—our bodies. We perceive our bodies as objects (Representations), but we also experience them from within, as acts of will (such as when you have the experience of wanting to move your arm). Schopenhauer believed our individual wills are part of a universal Will. This Will is an underlying force of nature, with no intelligence or aims of its own. By reflecting on our own will, we can come into contact with the Universe, and the basic energies that flow through it.

Both Kant and Schopenhauer said that there are limits to our knowledge of the external world, but thought we could say something about what is beyond these limits.

Our experience of the world is based on the **limitations** of our sense perceptions and our understanding. It is **impossible to know** how the world actually is **in itself** (see pp.60–61).

There are **universal moral laws**. What is **wrong for everybody else** must be **wrong for me** also (see pp.128 and p.140).

If we do whatever we want all the time, we are not **exercising free will**. We are **slaves to our impulses** and are not acting freely.

To appreciate a work of **art**, we must not base our judgment on **personal preferences** (see p.187).

Knowledge begins with **the senses**, proceeds then to the **understanding**, and **ends with reason**.

Immanuel Kant

EXPLORED THE LIMITS OF HUMAN KNOWLEDGE

Immanuel Kant is universally regarded as one of the greatest Western philosophers. He is known for bringing together the traditions of empiricism (the view that knowledge comes from experience) and rationalism (the view that knowledge comes from reasoning). His single unified theory of knowledge is an attempt to set the boundaries of what can be known.

Kant was born in 1724 in Königsberg in the German kingdom of Prussia (a city that has since been renamed Kaliningrad, and is now a part of Russia). His parents, who were devout Christians, provided him with a good education. He attended the University of Königsberg in 1740 where he enrolled as a student of theology (the study of religious belief), but he was also interested in mathematics and physics. Six years later, when his father died, he left his university to help his family, taking work as a private tutor. He returned to the university in 1755, and in the same year, he received his doctorate in philosophy. In 1770 he became a professor of metaphysics and logic at the University of Königsberg.

AN ACADEMIC LIFE

Compared to some other philosophers, Kant's everyday life was uneventful and routine. Yet the brilliance of his lectures made him very popular with his students.

LIKE CLOCKWORK ▶
Kant was known to follow a strict routine every day. His neighbors could set their watches by his daily walk.

He built a reputation as a leading academic, and became internationally famous during his lifetime.

Kant's first published work, *Thoughts on the True Estimation of Living Forces* (1747), was about the nature of space and physical force. But it wasn't until many years later that Kant wrote the book that would seal his place as one of the greatest philosophers in history, *Critique of Pure Reason* (1781). In this work Kant explained that since reality can only be experienced through the use of the senses and human understanding, there are limits to what we can know about the world. Kant was also deeply interested in the nature of morality. In *Groundwork of the Metaphysics of Morals* (1785), he argued that morality is grounded in reason and moral law.

Kant continued to write on philosophy until shortly before his death in 1804. His contributions on various subjects would have a lasting effect on many of the Western thinkers that followed him.

◀ COMPANY FOR DINNER
Kant's books have been described as difficult to read, but the man himself was an amusing speaker, and a master of sparkling conversation. He loved to have company, and rarely dined alone.

Is knowledge always based on facts?

We cannot claim to know something that is false, such as that the Moon is made of cheese. One of the requirements for knowledge is that whatever is claimed to be known must be true (see pp.48–49). In the 1800s, philosophers in the US began to question the nature of truth, and whether truth, and the knowledge it provides, has to be based on facts.

For much of its history, philosophy relied on what is called a "correspondence theory of truth." In this theory, a statement is true if it corresponds (matches up) to a fact—something that is consistent with reality and that can be proven with evidence. If somebody claims to know that Mount Everest is the tallest mountain on Earth, they are entitled to claim this as knowledge because it matches facts that can be found in the world.

PRAGMATISM

The correspondence theory of truth was challenged in the late 1800s by a new approach to philosophy known as pragmatism, which began in the US. At the heart of this philosophy is the idea that something is true because it is useful. Three of the most important early American pragmatists were Charles Sanders Peirce, William James, and John Dewey.

Peirce, the founder of pragmatism, thought that a lot of philosophical debate went into deciding whether something was true or not. But most of the time, all we really need is a satisfactory explanation. If we believe something, and it works for us, it doesn't really matter if it is an accurate picture of reality.

William James argued that truth is something that happens to an idea—a fact is made true if it makes a practical difference to our lives. If a person is lost in a wood, and they believe that the path before them will take them out of the wood, that is more useful than believing it won't and just staying where they are.

John Dewey saw ideas as neither true nor false, but instead as tools that help or hinder us in our lives. We test these ideas in the world, and if they prove to be useful, we accept them. For Dewey, the point of having ideas is practical problem-solving—knowledge serves a functional purpose.

PERSPECTIVISM

At much the same time that pragmatism was beginning in the US, the German philosopher Friedrich Nietzsche put forward a different idea about truth. He wrote: "There are no facts; there are only interpretations." This view was known as perspectivism. In rejecting the idea that truths line up with facts, Nietzsche was saying that what you think is true actually is true. We can all have

We must focus on problems that are stopping us from reaching our goals, rather than **minor issues** that have no **practical effect** on our lives.

When **ideas no longer work** for us we must **discard them** and come up with something new.

our own perspectives on the world, and are free to choose which truths to believe and which to ignore.

The 20th-century American philosopher Richard Rorty argued that what is claimed as knowledge by one community can be different for another community. We should not worry about a "Truth with a capital T" that applies to everyone. We must make our own truths by talking to one another, and then standing in solidarity with each other on things we agree about.

Some argue that this is an optimistic view. Truth and knowledge may be no more than perspectives, but we let loose dangerous views if we aren't careful. And if no view is superior to any other, then perspectivism itself is no better than a belief in Truth with a capital T.

▲ STANDING TOGETHER
Young people around the globe have come together to protest government policies on climate change. Rorty said that as there is no absolute truth that we must live by, the best that we can do is to make a stand with others about the things that we believe in.

USEFUL KNOWLEDGE
According to pragmatism, knowledge is a tool that we use to fix problems. Only useful ideas should be kept; others should be discarded.

We are always looking for **more useful tools** that will solve our problems more quickly or efficiently.

We solve problems by **actively getting involved**. Knowledge must be something that we **participate in**, rather than just observe.

Ideas are tools, and each problem we face requires us to select a suitable tool to solve it.

THE MIND

The philosophy of mind explores what a mind is, and what it means to have one. Philosophers have debated whether the mind is something separate from the body, or whether it is linked to our physical form. They have also examined whether we can know what is going on in other people's minds, and if robots and computers will ever be able to think like humans.

What is a mind?

For 2,500 years, philosophers have wondered about the mind—the thing that actually allows humans to wonder. Philosophers have disagreed about the exact nature of the mind, but it is often thought of today as the private place where a person's identity—their hopes, beliefs, ideas, experiences, perceptions, and memories—exists.

THE MIND

For a long time, the mind as we think of it today was known as the soul. For the ancient Greeks, the soul was a life-giving force—the difference between being alive and dead. It wasn't until the 1600s that the idea of the mind as the location of a person's sense of self began to take hold. In the 1900s, some philosophers stopped thinking of the mind as a thing altogether, arguing instead that the mind was to be found in the behavior of a person, or the functions that happen in the brain.

In the 4th century BCE, the ancient Greek philosopher Plato wrote in his *Phaedo* that the soul is indestructible and immortal. He believed that

> The idea of an immortal soul, separate from the body, eventually became a core belief of Judaism, Christianity, and Islam.

a soul temporarily inhabits a body until death, when it moves into another body. His student Aristotle disagreed, arguing that the soul couldn't exist or act without its body. For Aristotle, the body is made of matter, and the soul, while not physical, animates that matter. Therefore, the soul would cease to exist after the body's death.

THE IMMATERIAL MIND

In the 1600s, French thinker René Descartes argued that the mind is an immaterial substance (a substance not made of matter) inhabiting a physical body. He pointed out that doubting is something that minds do, and so if he was able to doubt the existence of his

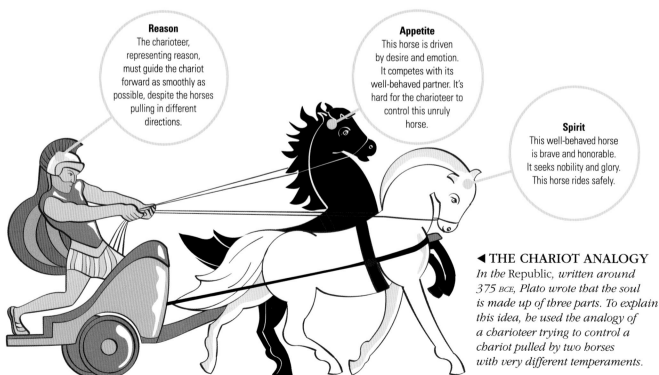

Reason
The charioteer, representing reason, must guide the chariot forward as smoothly as possible, despite the horses pulling in different directions.

Appetite
This horse is driven by desire and emotion. It competes with its well-behaved partner. It's hard for the charioteer to control this unruly horse.

Spirit
This well-behaved horse is brave and honorable. It seeks nobility and glory. This horse rides safely.

◀ **THE CHARIOT ANALOGY**
In the Republic, *written around 375 BCE, Plato wrote that the soul is made up of three parts. To explain this idea, he used the analogy of a charioteer trying to control a chariot pulled by two horses with very different temperaments.*

But what then am I? A **thing that thinks.**

RENÉ DESCARTES, *Meditations on First Philosophy* (1641)

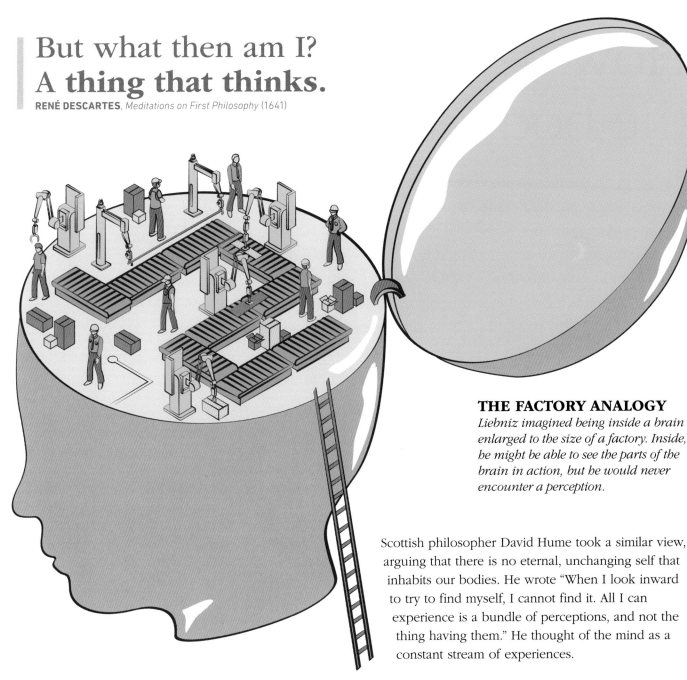

THE FACTORY ANALOGY
Liebniz imagined being inside a brain enlarged to the size of a factory. Inside, he might be able to see the parts of the brain in action, but he would never encounter a perception.

Scottish philosopher David Hume took a similar view, arguing that there is no eternal, unchanging self that inhabits our bodies. He wrote "When I look inward to try to find myself, I cannot find it. All I can experience is a bundle of perceptions, and not the thing having them." He thought of the mind as a constant stream of experiences.

own mind, then his mind must, in fact, exist. He later went on to describe himself as a "thinking thing." After Descartes, the concept of the mind began to diverge from the concept of the soul.

The 17th-century German philosopher Gottfried Leibniz supported the view that the mind should be thought of as immaterial. He used the analogy of a brain enlarged to the size of a factory to show that the mind's perceptions cannot be explained by watching the physical brain at work. He believed this meant there must be something else at work beyond the physical.

CHANGING MINDS

In the West, the mind is associated with the sense of self, but Buddhists believe that there is no such thing as a permanent, unchanging self. The 18th-century

NOUN OR VERB?

Philosophers began to consider the mind in a very different way in the 1900s. They believed that it was wrong to think of the mind as a noun, or a "thing." A group of philosophers known as behaviorists argued instead that the mind is a verb—it is the behaviors that a person carries out. For behaviorists, the mind is something that people do, not something that they have.

Other philosophers, known as functionalists, agreed that the mind was not a thing, but for a different reason. For functionalists, the mind is nothing other than the functions which occur inside the brain, such as thought and memory. Both the behaviorist and functionalist approaches imply that any system as complex as the brain, such as the software of a robot, could also have a mind, not just humans.

How do the mind and the body interact?

The nature of the relationship between the mind and the body has been so frequently debated that it has become known as the mind–body problem. Some thinkers have argued that the mind is something separate from the body, and capable of existing on its own after death. Others have argued that a mind must be linked to a body, and can only exist for as long as the body survives. Many modern thinkers suggest that what we call mind is nothing more than what goes on in our brains.

Debates about how the mind interacts with the body that it appears to inhabit, particularly the physical processes of the brain, have been going on for thousands of years. When early philosophers discussed the subject, they used the term "soul" (see p.68). But they were still talking about what later philosophers would call "mind"—that part of us that is considered to hold the core of our identity, or our sense of self.

SEPARATE MINDS

The idea that the mind exists independently from the body is a form of substance dualism—the belief that there are two kinds of substances in the world: physical things made of matter, and mental things that are not made of matter. Early ideas about substance dualism developed in both Western and Eastern philosophy in around the 5th–4th centuries BCE. The ancient Greek

❔ THE FLOATING PERSON

Ibn Sīnā's thought experiment examined whether a person unaware of anything else would still be aware of their own existence. Ibn Sīnā believed that they would still have a sense of self, and that this must be made from a different substance than the body.

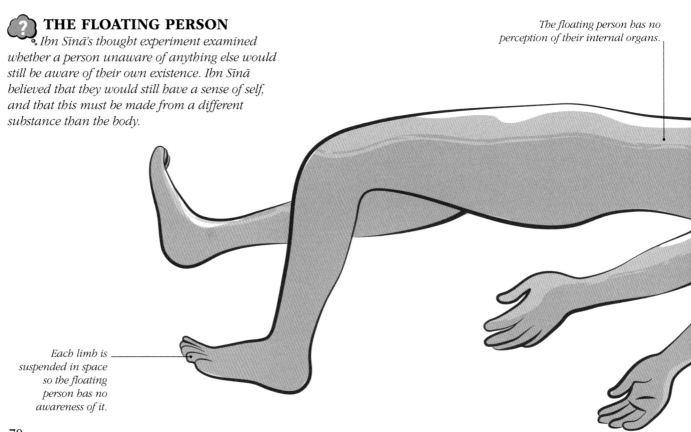

The floating person has no perception of their internal organs.

Each limb is suspended in space so the floating person has no awareness of it.

thinker Plato, and Indian philosophers of the Samkhya Hindu tradition, suggested that the mind inhabits the body as a separate independent substance.

Much later, in the 11th century, the Muslim Persian philosopher Ibn Sīnā came up with a thought experiment to demonstrate that the mind must exist, and that it must be separate from the body. He imagined a person who had sprung into existence, fully formed, floating in an empty space. In this experiment, the person has no working senses, so they have no way of knowing about the external world, or even of the existence of their own bodies. Ibn Sīnā argued that this person would still be aware that they had a personal identity, or a mind. And because this floating person has no knowledge of their body, this mind cannot be a part of that body, and must be a separate substance. The 17th-century French philosopher René Descartes made a similar argument, as he was able to prove his own mind's existence even when he couldn't prove the existence of his own body (see p.54).

TURNING THOUGHTS INTO ACTIONS

If the mind is separate and different from the body, how does the mind cause things to happen within the body? For example, how does the thought "I want to move my arm" actually cause the arm to move? Princess Elisabeth of Bohemia wrote a letter to René Descartes, asking a similar question. Descartes wasn't able to give her an answer that she found acceptable, but many later thinkers also attempted to answer the question.

How does this woman's thought cause the action she performs?

I WISH TO MOVE MY ARM.

▲ THE INTERACTION PROBLEM
Philosophers who claim that the mind is separate from the body are faced with the problem of explaining how thoughts, which are not physical, can cause physical actions.

The 17th-century German philosopher Gottfried Leibniz suggested that every time we wish to move our bodies, God translates this desire into movement, making sure that our minds and bodies work in harmony. But this solution has two problems. The first is that if this is true, then our minds don't actually cause bodily actions— God does—so our minds don't really have any effect on our bodies at all. The second problem is that if God turns our thoughts into actions, this would mean that God is involved in all of our bad acts, such as using a weapon to injure somebody.

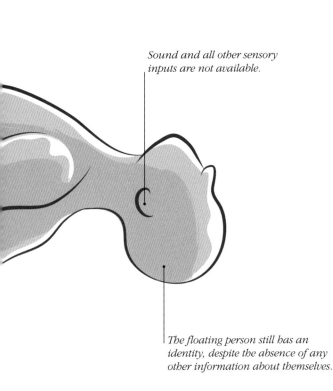

Sound and all other sensory inputs are not available.

The floating person still has an identity, despite the absence of any other information about themselves.

PRINCESS ELISABETH OF BOHEMIA

Princess Elisabeth of Bohemia (1618–1680) didn't write any philosophical works of her own. However, she made huge contributions to philosophy through her correspondence with the thinker René Descartes. In letters written to each other between 1643 and 1650, they debated a variety of topics including the mind–body problem, the freedom of human will, and what it means to govern well.

Thomas Henry Huxley, a 19th-century English biologist and philosopher, came up with an ingenious answer to the mind–body problem. He suggested that the mind is like steam that passes through the whistle of a steam train to make a noise—it's a by-product of the train's engine, rather than the cause of the train's movement. In a similar way, the mind is a by-product of brain activity, rather than a cause of brain activity. For Huxley, bodily movements are entirely explained by physical processes in the brain—the mind isn't involved at all.

PHYSICALISM

Huxley's theory that the mind is a by-product of physical processes is part of a viewpoint in the philosophy of mind that is known as physicalism. For physicalists, only one substance exists—physical substance. Anything that appears to be "mental" can be explained by physical means. The mind is not a "thing" that exists in itself. Several philosophers have argued that minds are identical in some way to brains, or at least are nothing else other than brains.

The 20th-century English physicalist Gilbert Ryle referred to the idea of a mind causing a body to move as a "ghost in the machine." He called looking for a mind that exists beyond physical processes a "category mistake." To explain what he meant, Ryle used an analogy. Imagine that your friend asks you to show them a university. You show them the colleges, the laboratories, and the students. It would then be a mistake for your friend to demand: "I have seen all these

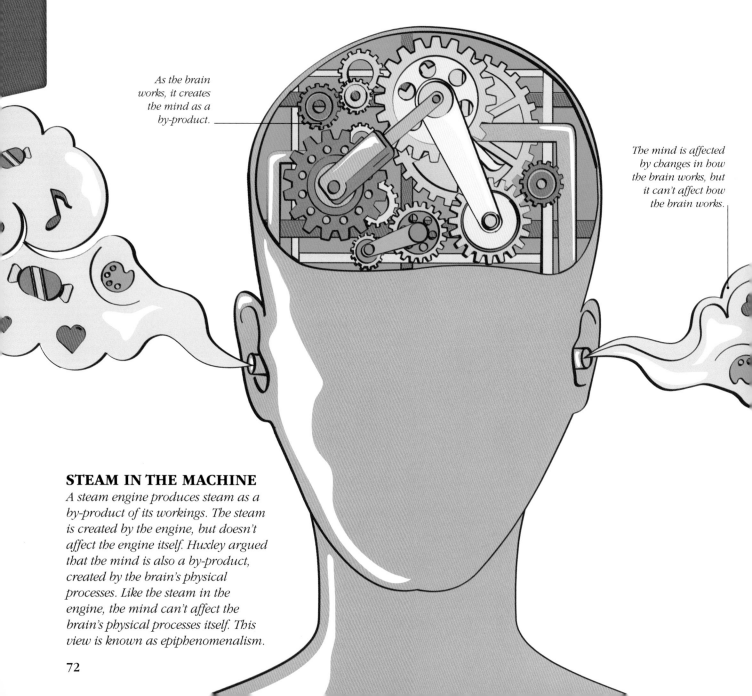

As the brain works, it creates the mind as a by-product.

The mind is affected by changes in how the brain works, but it can't affect how the brain works.

STEAM IN THE MACHINE

A steam engine produces steam as a by-product of its workings. The steam is created by the engine, but doesn't affect the engine itself. Huxley argued that the mind is also a by-product, created by the brain's physical processes. Like the steam in the engine, the mind can't affect the brain's physical processes itself. This view is known as epiphenomenalism.

things, but now show me the university". There is nothing that is the university over and above the colleges, laboratories, and so on. In the same way, if you ask: "Where is the mind, over and above the workings of the brain?" you are making the same category mistake. There is nothing else to point to. You are treating the mind as though it were a further object, over and above the behaviors shown by the brain.

University classroom

University laboratory

🗨 **CATEGORY MISTAKE**

Ryle likened the search for a "mind" separate from its body with searching for a "university" over and above its classrooms, laboratories, and other buildings.

THE MIND

PROPERTY DUALISM

Another theory about the relationship between the mind and the body is known as property dualism. It claims that there is only one substance in the world—matter— but that this matter can have different properties. This idea

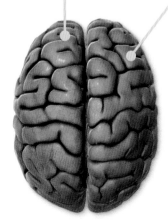

mental properties. This potential is locked inside every atom, everywhere, not just in the ones that compose brains. The theory of property dualism still doesn't resolve the question of how our minds—what the property dualists would see as the "mental properties" of our brains—interact with our bodies. And if moving an arm can be explained by the physical properties of the brain, what contribution do mental properties make to that movement, or in fact to anything at all?

Is mind nothing more than the workings of the brain? Or is the mind a separate substance? Or a collection of mental properties? Philosophy has no definite answers to these questions, which is why it is a topic that continues to fascinate philosophers of mind to this day.

Physical
The brain is made of different types of physical matter including cells, water, fat, and blood vessels that tinge it the color red.

Mental
The brain has mental properties as well as physical ones, including emotions, memories, and desires.

was first put forward by the 17th-century Dutch philosopher Spinoza, and today it is supported by the Australian philosopher of mind David Chalmers. Property dualism says that the brain has physical properties—for example, it has a wrinkled surface and three-quarters of it is water. However, it also has mental properties—it has experiences. According to Chalmers, all matter—even a rock or a lake—has the potential for

◀ **THE MATTER OF BRAINS**

Property dualists believe that the brain is made of matter, but that this matter has two properties—physical and mental properties. Some philosophers believe that all matter in the Universe, not just brains, is to some degree conscious. This belief is known as panpsychism.

DESCARTES AND THE QUEEN
When Descartes was invited to tutor Queen Christina of Sweden in 1649, she insisted that he begin teaching at 5 am. But Descartes was used to sleeping very late into the morning. When he caught pneumonia, he blamed it on this change to his routine, as well as the Swedish climate. The illness led to his death a year later.

No more **useful inquiry** can be proposed than that which seeks to determine **the nature and scope** of **human knowledge**.

René Descartes

RETURNED TO FIRST PRINCIPLES

By questioning the basic principles of what we can know, French philosopher René Descartes set aside the philosophical tradition of the past. He embraced new scientific ways of thinking about the world, beginning a new era of modern philosophy.

René Descartes was born in La Haye en Touraine, France in 1596. His mother died within a year of his birth, and he was raised by his grandmother and his great-uncle. Descartes' father sent him to study at the Royal College in La Flèche, France in 1606. Though his health was fragile, Descartes excelled at school, particularly in mathematics. His family wanted him to become a lawyer, so he studied law at the University of Poitiers. But after finishing his degree, he became a soldier for a time instead. Though he was never involved in any fighting, he did get to travel widely across Europe.

THE FIRST CERTAINTY

During his varied education, Descartes heard many conflicting viewpoints. This led him to question what he believed, and whether he could ever know anything for certain. Eventually, he developed a theory of knowledge based on the statement "I think, therefore I am." Descartes argued that the first thing he could be certain of was the fact that he existed. He called this "the first certainty."

In *Discourse on the Method* (1637), Descartes explained that from this starting point, knowledge can be achieved through reasoning alone (a view that would eventually be known as rationalism). His most important book, *Meditations on First Philosophy* (1641), argued that we gain knowledge on a variety of subjects, from the nature of the mind to the existence of God, just by reasoning.

In 1649 Queen Christina of Sweden invited Descartes to tutor her. The harsh Swedish winter made him seriously ill, and he died in Stockholm in 1650. But Descartes' ideas had already kickstarted a new debate on the nature of knowledge that would last for the next three centuries.

The **certainty** that is found in **mathematics** should be applicable to **the sciences and philosophy**.

There are two kinds of substance: **mental and material**. The **mind, or soul,** is separate from the **body** (see p.71).

While it is possible for us to **doubt many things**, the fact that we are doubting, and **therefore thinking**, is the **proof of our existence** (see pp.68–69).

I find within myself the clear and distinct idea of a **perfect God.** For something to be perfect, it must exist, therefore **God exists.** (see p.54).

PLATO ▶
(c.429–347 BCE)
Ancient Greek philosopher Plato wrote extensively about the "psyche" (soul, mind, or spirit), claiming that it is immortal, and separate from the body.

"The human soul is immortal."

"What makes a body living is not the dimensions which make it a body... but something more excellent like a soul."

▲ THOMAS AQUINAS
(c.1225–1274)
Italian Catholic priest Aquinas argued that the "anima" (soul) animates the human body to make it a living organism.

In philosophy, dualism is the belief that reality is formed of two substances. Mind–body dualism is the view that humans are composed of a physical body, and a nonphysical mind.

MIND–BODY DUALISM
versus
PHYSICALISM

The view that only physical things can possibly exist is known as physicalism. According to physicalists, the mind is not a separate substance from the body. Mental activity can be explained by physical activity within the brain.

"Minds are not merely ghosts harnessed to machines."

JACOB MOLESCHOTT ▶
(1822–1893)
Dutch-Italian philosopher Moleschott argued that mental activity could be explained scientifically. He held that thoughts in the mind are the product of chemicals in the brain.

"A force unconnected with matter... is an utterly empty conception."

▲ GILBERT RYLE (1900–1976)
The English philosopher Ryle criticized the dualistic idea of the mind inhabiting the body, saying this would be like a "ghost in the machine."

▼ RENÉ DESCARTES (1596–1650)
Believing that minds and bodies are formed of two separate substances, French philosopher Descartes described our minds as perfect, and immortal parts of our beings.

"It is certain that I am really distinct from my body, and can exist without it."

"Perception, and that which depends upon it, cannot be explained through mechanical means."

GOTTFRIED LEIBNIZ (1646–1716) ▲
German thinker Leibniz said that the mind couldn't be explained by the mechanical workings of the body, and so must be separate from it.

GEORGE BERKELEY ▶
(1685–1753)
Irish philosopher Berkeley insisted that only two types of thing exist—perceptions of the world, including perceptions of our own bodies, and the minds that do the perceiving.

"This perceiving, active being is what I call mind, spirit, soul, or myself."

▼ U.T. PLACE (1924–2000)
English philosopher and psychologist Place developed the identity theory of mind, which says that states and processes of the mind are identical to states and processes of the brain.

"Consciousness is a process in the brain."

"... your brain can go from a state of being conscious to a state of being unconscious, depending on the behavior of the molecules."

JOHN SEARLE (born 1932) ▲
American thinker Searle explained that mental events (events that happen within the mind) are actually the products of biological interactions inside the brain.

DANIEL DENNETT ▶
(born 1942)
American philosopher and scientist Dennett argued that all thoughts and mental activity are produced by the brain, which gathers information from the senses.

"It is not so much that we, using our brains, spin our yarns, as that our brains, using yarns, spin us."

TEACHING STUDENTS
In this illustrated page from The Canon of Medicine, *Ibn Sīnā is instructing people on how best to bathe, as well as on how to play music—some of the things he thought were needed for a healthy life.*

No **knowledge** is acquired except through the **study** of its causes and **beginnings.**

Ibn Sīnā

ISLAMIC PHILOSOPHER AND SCIENTIST

Ibn Sīnā (also known as Avicenna) was a man of many talents. Living in the 10th century, during a period known as the Islamic Golden Age, he was an expert in medicine and astronomy, as well as one of the most influential philosophers of the medieval world.

Ibn Sīnā was born in c.980 CE near Bukhara, part of the Persian Empire (now in present-day Uzbekistan). He was an exceptionally gifted student, and at 10 years of age he became a Quran Hafiz, meaning that he had memorized the whole religious text of Islam. He also became renowned for his medical expertise, and when he was 18, he was summoned to cure the ailments of Nuh ibn Mansur, the Sultan of Bukhara. This gave him access to the sultan's extraordinary library, where he was able to read Arabic translations of books of Indian and Greek philosophy. These included the works of Aristotle, whose ideas influenced him greatly.

With these resources, Ibn Sīnā conceived the idea of the Floating Person, claiming that the mind was separate from the body—he did this several hundred years before René Descartes had a similar theory.

WRITER AND STARGAZER

Ibn Sīnā wrote hundreds of books on many subjects, the first of which was published when he was 21. His scientific study, *The Canon of Medicine* (1025), was the standard medical textbook in European universities until the mid-1600s. His major contribution to philosophy was *The Book of Healing* (1027), in which he recommended philosophy as a remedy to rid the soul of ignorance in the same way that medicine cures the body of illness. Ibn Sīnā also invented an instrument for observing the stars, which led him to discover that Venus was closer to the Sun than to Earth.

Ibn Sīnā died in 1037 CE, and is buried in Hamedan, Iran. He is considered one of the most important medieval philosophers, whose influence spread from the Islamic world through to the West.

The "**Floating Person**" demonstrates human **self-awareness** and the existence of the **soul** in the absence of the senses and a physical body (see pp.70–71).

In a **finite universe**, one that has a beginning, all events in reality can be traced back to an **uncaused cause**—God.

God is a "**necessary existent**"—it would be impossible for God not to exist.

The **nature of God** is **different** from that of **humans**. God is made of a simple substance that cannot be divided.

Can I know that you're thinking?

We have access to our own private thoughts and minds, but we don't have the same access to the thoughts and minds of others. Because of this, how can we be sure other people have thoughts and minds at all? In philosophy, this question is known as the problem of other minds.

The French philosopher René Descartes wrote about the problem of other minds in his *Meditations*, published in 1641. Descartes wrote that his thoughts were known to him from within, but he had no way of knowing for sure whether other people on the street had minds like his. They might simply be nonthinking, nonfeeling machines made of flesh and bone. This idea can be taken even further—for all you know, other people might not have minds at all. This is a form of skepticism, which is the view that we can't know things with any certainty. With no direct evidence for the existence of other people's minds, you might even go so far as to conclude that you are the only thinking person in the world.

Some philosophers who came after Descartes have entertained similar ideas. The modern Australian philosopher David Chalmers wrote that we have no "experience meter" to tell us if anybody else is having inner experiences. We can be certain of our own experience, as we can feel our own emotions, desires, and pains. But when it comes to other

◀ BEING A BAT
The 20th-century American philosopher Thomas Nagel asked, "What is it like to be a bat?" He concluded that we can never know because we can't escape our own perspective.

80

INNER THOUGHTS
While other people show signs of enjoyment, they may not be having any kind of internal experience. The person in the yellow top can only be sure that they themselves have a mind—not that anyone else does.

people, although we can observe their behavior, we simply can't be sure whether they have these inner experiences, too.

You have no way of being able to tell whether or not your friends are "philosophical zombies"—nonthinking, nonfeeling beings who act just like normal humans. They might carry out the same behaviors that human beings do, but with no inner lives and no minds of their own. One of these philosophical zombies might say "Ouch" if a heavy item falls on its feet, even if it feels no pain or other internal sensations.

MIND IS BEHAVIOR

Some philosophers don't really see the problem of other minds as a problem at all. A group of philosophers known as behaviorists believe that the mind is nothing other than the behaviors it carries out (see p.69), so to experience another person's behavior is to experience their mind. The ideas of the behaviorists have fallen out of fashion, but in our ordinary interactions with others, we infer from people's outward behavior that they do have minds and sensations like ours.

The 20th-century Austrian philosopher Ludwig Wittgenstein came up with a famous answer to the problem of other minds. He reasoned that even a solipsist (a person who is convinced that they are the only thinking person in the world) uses language. Wittgenstein argued that in order to learn a language, we need other people with whom we can cross-reference the meaning and usage of words. We can't

PHILOSOPHICAL ZOMBIES

We can see other people carrying out seemingly human behaviors, but we can't tell if they have an authentic inner mind that directs these actions. Other "people" might be philosophical zombies, functioning without thoughts.

define and develop a language by ourselves. Creating and using a language isn't an activity that can be achieved by just one person. In Wittgenstein's view, language relies on other people to work, so there must be other people with minds in the world for it to exist.

THINK FOR YOURSELF

Imagine a red object. If you are color-blind, you might experience redness differently from other people. But even if you aren't color-blind, is there any way to tell whether what you experience as "red" is the same experience that others have? It's impossible to get into another person's mind to find out. Wittgenstein argued that there must be something in common between things that are red, otherwise we would never be able to agree on what red is.

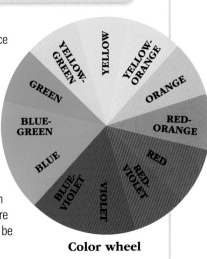

Color wheel

Could a machine ever think?

We live in an age of artificial intelligence (AI), with voice-controlled smart phones, driverless cars, and computers that can beat world-class chess players. For philosophers, the development of artificially intelligent computer systems raises questions about what it means to be considered an intelligent being.

In the 1950s, British mathematician Alan Turing considered how machines could be appropriately tested for their intelligence or their ability to "think." He devised a test in which a human interviewer ask questions to another human and a machine, but is unable to see either of them. The interviewer must try to detect which is the human and which is the machine based on their replies. If the interviewer can't tell which is which, it may be possible to conclude that the machine is capable of thinking, and that it has passed the Turing Test. Each year a competition, known as the Loebner Prize, is held to find the computer program that interviewers take the longest time to recognize as a machine. To date, no program has fooled the interviewers for more than 25 minutes.

COMPUTER INTELLIGENCE

Though no machine has yet been able to pass the Turing Test, this test only proves that a machine can simulate intelligent behavior. It doesn't say anything about whether that machine can be said to have a "mind." Some philosophers have suggested that instead of focusing on behavior, we should look at what is happening "inside." In 1980 the American philosopher John Searle argued that a machine can, for all intents and purposes, look like it's thinking. But inside it has no understanding comparable to that of a human. His

The interviewer asks questions and analyzes the answers.

The machine responds according to its programming.

Machine

Interviewer

Human

The human responds in a conversational way.

▲ THE TURING TEST
The test assesses the ability of a machine to imitate human conversation. Whether the computer gives the correct answers or not doesn't matter. The test is a measure of how well the machine can answer in a humanlike way.

> **May not machines** carry out something which ought to **be described as thinking**?
>
> **ALAN TURING**, *Computing Machinery and Intelligence* (1950)

thought experiment, The Chinese Room, describes a person locked in a room receiving questions written in Chinese, a language they do not understand. With the help of an instruction manual, however, they are able to respond correctly, though they will never know what the questions or the answers actually mean. Searle argues this is just what it is like inside a computer. It responds according to a step-by-step process, but it can't be said to understand like a human. For humans, most mental states are created in response to something outside of us—tasting ice cream, experiencing the weather, hearing the singing of birds outside, or reading a book, for example. Searle refers to this as "aboutness." But nothing that happens inside The Chinese Room seems to be about anything outside of it. The human in the room is not able to form any relevant belief about the world outside, from the questions put to them.

ARTIFICIAL OR ORGANIC?

From the late 1900s onward, a group of philosophers known as functionalists have rejected Searle's view of what it is possible for a mechanical machine to understand. Functionalists believe it is only the function (the task) of an object that matters, not what the object is made from. For example, a key can be any shape or material, but as long as it unlocks an object, it is still a key. Functionalists argue it is equally possible for the

same mental states (such as desires, hopes, and emotions) to happen in different physical bodies. For them, the artificial hardware of an android is potentially just as capable of having a mind as an organic brain inside the head of a human.

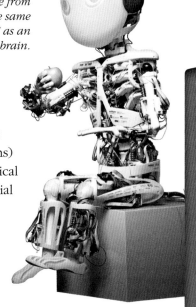

HUMANOID ROBOT ▶
Functionalists argue that a robot with a "brain" made from metal and plastic has the same potential to "think" as an organic human brain.

THE MIND

A series of questions, written in Chinese, are posted through a gap onto a desk. These represent **queries input** into a computer.

The person doesn't understand the questions but follows a step-by-step procedure, like those used by **computer processors**, making it possible for them to answer correctly.

THE CHINESE ROOM
Searle's thought experiment of The Chinese Room compares a person translating an unknown language with what goes on inside a computer. It implies that machines are not capable of actual understanding.

On the desk is a manual which gives instructions for what to write when a particular symbol or set of symbols appear, like a **computer program**.

The person passes their responses outside, through another gap. This represents the **information output** of a computer.

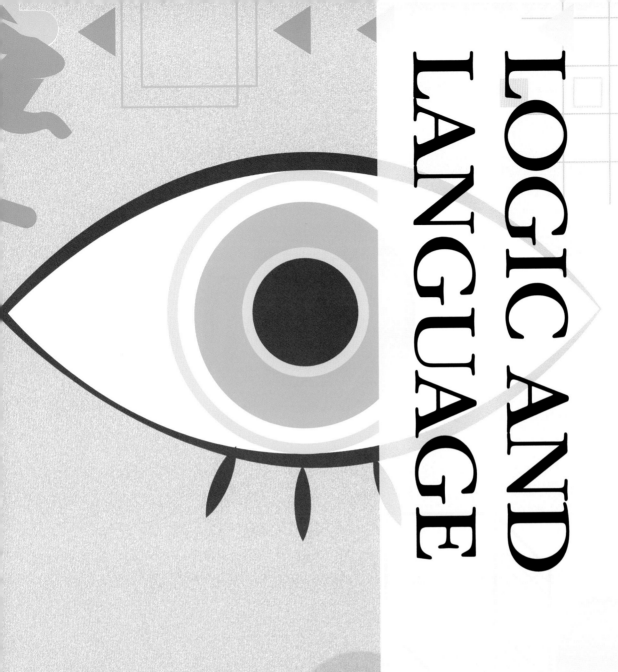

LOGIC AND LANGUAGE

To support the truth of an idea, we may use an argument—a set of reasons that acts as evidence for our claim. Logic is the branch of philosophy that studies these arguments. It has identified many types of arguments, both good and faulty. In the early 1900s, philosophers of logic began to apply its rules to language more generally. Later thinkers have focused on how we use language in everyday life.

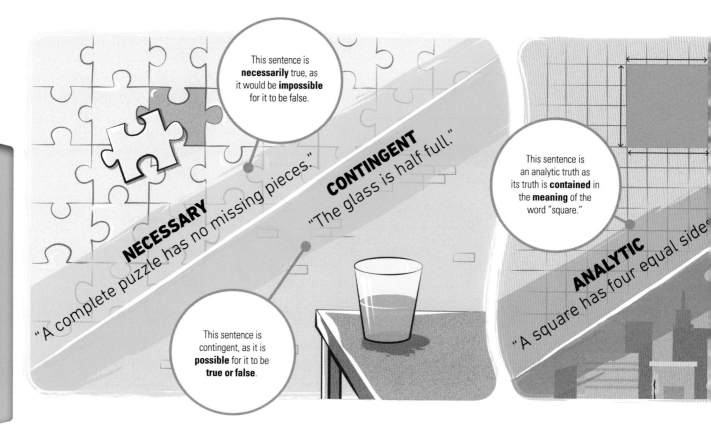

This sentence is **necessarily** true, as it would be **impossible** for it to be false.

NECESSARY

"A complete puzzle has no missing pieces."

CONTINGENT

"The glass is half full."

This sentence is contingent, as it is **possible** for it to be **true or false**.

This sentence is an analytic truth as its truth is **contained** in the **meaning** of the word "square."

ANALYTIC

"A square has four equal sides"

What is truth?

In logic, truth can be thought of as a property of sentences and the beliefs expressed by sentences. This means that sentences, and the beliefs that they contain, can be said to be either true or untrue. Philosophers have classified truths in various ways.

When philosophers ask about the truth of a statement, they ask several different kinds of questions. They question whether the statement is necessarily true. They question its language and meaning. And they question the role of reasoning and experience in determining the statement's truth.

TYPES OF TRUTH

The first question philosophers ask is whether a sentence must be true. Is there any way that it could be false? A sentence that must be true is known as a necessary truth (see top left above). Sentences that can be either true or false are known as contingent truths (see top left below).

A second way of asking about truth looks at the language of a sentence. It is possible for some sentences to be true by definition—their truth can be determined by looking at the meaning of the words they contain.

Sentences that are true by definition are known as analytic truths (see top middle above). Other sentences are not true by definition, and philosophers call these kinds of truths synthetic truths (see top middle below).

Finally, philosophers classify truths in terms of how we come to know them. It is possible to determine the truth of some sentences just by using our powers of reasoning alone. These are known in philosophy as *a priori* truths (see top right above). But there are sentences that require us to look outside of ourselves to see if they are true. These kinds of truths are known as *a posteriori* truths (see top right below).

IDEAS AND FACTS

In the early 1700s, the Scottish philosopher David Hume made a distinction between what he called "relations of ideas" and "matters of fact." Relations of ideas are statements that relate to abstract ideas. These can be

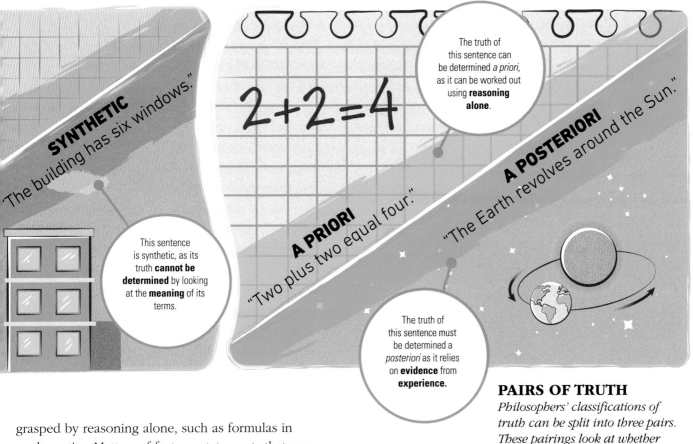

SYNTHETIC
"The building has six windows."

This sentence is synthetic, as its truth **cannot be determined** by looking at the **meaning** of its terms.

$$2+2=4$$

A PRIORI
"Two plus two equal four."

The truth of this sentence can be determined *a priori*, as it can be worked out using **reasoning alone**.

A POSTERIORI
"The Earth revolves around the Sun."

The truth of this sentence must be determined *a posteriori* as it relies on **evidence** from **experience**.

LOGIC AND LANGUAGE

grasped by reasoning alone, such as formulas in mathematics. Matters of fact are statements that say something about what we can experience. Hume suggested that these two types of statements are understood in different ways. Later some philosophers imagined this as a branching path, which has come to be known as "Hume's fork." On one branch of the path are relations of ideas, which are necessary, analytic, and *a priori*, while on the other are matters of fact that are contingent, synthetic, and *a posteriori*.

But other thinkers have questioned whether truths can be so neatly split. The 18th-century German philosopher Immanuel Kant believed that moral statements, such as "lying is wrong," are examples of synthetic statements—the word "lying" isn't defined as "wrong." But for Kant the truth of moral statements are known *a priori*—they can be understood just by thinking them through.

Until 1980 many philosophers believed that all necessary truths were knowable *a priori*. But then the philosopher Saul Kripke came up with a very influential argument that the sentence "water is H_2O" is both necessary and *a posteriori*. It is necessary—there is no possibility that water is not the same thing as H_2O—but this can only be understood through learning about science, specifically chemistry, so it must be *a posteriori*, known through experience.

PAIRS OF TRUTH
Philosophers' classifications of truth can be split into three pairs. These pairings look at whether truths are necessary or contingent, analytic or synthetic, and a priori *or* a posteriori.

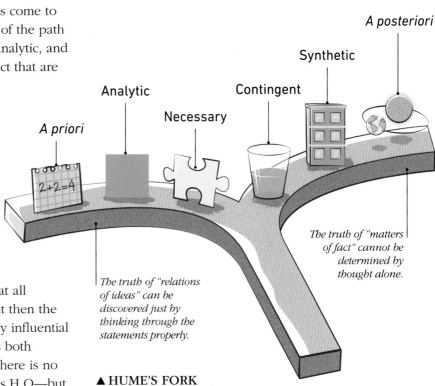

A posteriori

Synthetic

Analytic

Necessary

Contingent

A priori

The truth of "matters of fact" cannot be determined by thought alone.

The truth of "relations of ideas" can be discovered just by thinking through the statements properly.

▲ HUME'S FORK
Hume divided statements into two kinds: "relations of ideas" and "matters of fact." These statements split at a fork into two diverging branches based on their truth.

87

What makes a good argument?

In philosophy, an argument doesn't describe two people having a quarrel. A philosophical argument is a logical progression through a set of statements to reach a particular conclusion. There can be good arguments and bad arguments, but what makes one argument better than another?

An argument is made of several statements, known as "premises," that support a conclusion. A good argument is one in which the conclusion "follows" from its premises—meaning that if all of the premises are true, then the conclusion is justified. In a bad argument, the conclusion doesn't follow from the premises. There are two types of argument in logic: deductive arguments and inductive arguments.

DEDUCTIVE ARGUMENTS

In a deductive argument, if the premises are true, then the conclusion must also be true—there is no possibility that the conclusion could be false. The ancient Greek philosopher Aristotle was the first to study deductive logic. He came up with very simple deductive arguments known as syllogisms, such as the one below (see far left). A good deductive argument is said to be "valid."

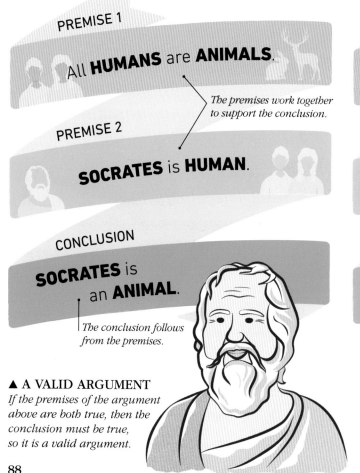

PREMISE 1

All **HUMANS** are **ANIMALS**.

The premises work together to support the conclusion.

PREMISE 2

SOCRATES is **HUMAN**.

CONCLUSION

SOCRATES is an **ANIMAL**.

The conclusion follows from the premises.

▲ **A VALID ARGUMENT**
If the premises of the argument above are both true, then the conclusion must be true, so it is a valid argument.

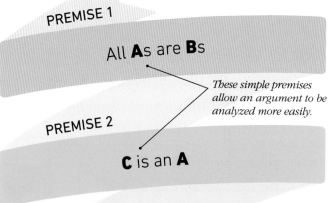

PREMISE 1

All **A**s are **B**s

These simple premises allow an argument to be analyzed more easily.

PREMISE 2

C is an **A**

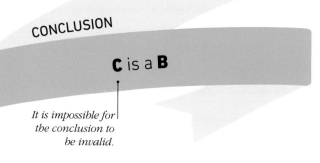

CONCLUSION

C is a **B**

It is impossible for the conclusion to be invalid.

▲ **LOGICAL FORM**
The logical form of the two deductive arguments on either side can be analyzed by replacing their content with letters. By doing this, it's possible to see that both arguments have the same logical structure.

Bad deductive arguments are said to be "invalid." In an invalid argument, there is a logically possible situation in which all of the premises are true but the conclusion drawn from them is false. Invalid deductive arguments are types of fallacies (see pp.90–91).

A valid deductive argument is only as good as the information fed into it. If just one of the premises is false, even if the argument is valid, the conclusion may also be false (see directly below). A valid argument in which all premises are true is a "sound" argument.

Philosophers of logic, known as logicians, analyze deductive arguments by replacing their contents. The 19th-century German logician Gottlob Frege replaced the content of deductive arguments with letters and symbols to see the logical "form" of these arguments. Analyzing this logical form made it easier to see whether the arguments were valid or invalid.

INDUCTIVE ARGUMENTS

Unlike deductive arguments, inductive arguments are based on an assumption that the future will be like the past. You might believe the next daffodil you see will be yellow because, in your experience, all other daffodils you have seen have been yellow.

ABDUCTIVE ARGUMENTS

The fictional detective Sherlock Holmes is often mistakenly believed to use deductive logic to solve his cases. But his conclusions are in fact based on inductive logic—he infers facts based on previous evidence. Holmes uses a specific type of inductive logic known as abduction. Abductive arguments make a "best guess" from available information. A doctor will use abduction to make a diagnosis based on the evidence provided by a patient's symptoms.

Sherlock Holmes

Inductive arguments can never be valid—even if their premises are true their conclusions might still turn out to be false. Not every daffodil that has ever flowered has been yellow. But a good inductive argument doesn't need to be valid. It just needs to be likely that the conclusion of an inductive argument is true if all of the premises are also true. A good inductive argument is known as a "strong" inductive argument.

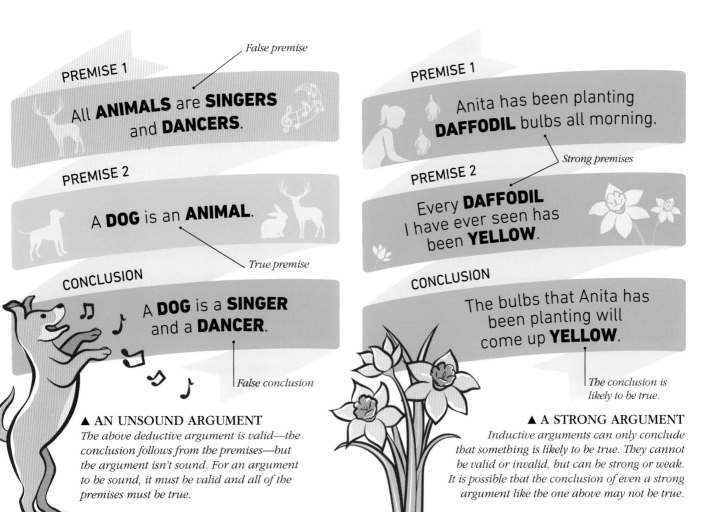

False premise

PREMISE 1

All **ANIMALS** are **SINGERS** and **DANCERS**.

PREMISE 2

A **DOG** is an **ANIMAL**.

True premise

CONCLUSION

A **DOG** is a **SINGER** and a **DANCER**.

False conclusion

▲ AN UNSOUND ARGUMENT
The above deductive argument is valid—the conclusion follows from the premises—but the argument isn't sound. For an argument to be sound, it must be valid and all of the premises must be true.

PREMISE 1

Anita has been planting **DAFFODIL** bulbs all morning.

Strong premises

PREMISE 2

Every **DAFFODIL** I have ever seen has been **YELLOW**.

CONCLUSION

The bulbs that Anita has been planting will come up **YELLOW**.

The conclusion is likely to be true.

▲ A STRONG ARGUMENT
Inductive arguments can only conclude that something is likely to be true. They cannot be valid or invalid, but can be strong or weak. It is possible that the conclusion of even a strong argument like the one above may not be true.

What is a fallacy?

Fallacies are patterns of faulty reasoning. They have so often been mistaken for patterns of correct reasoning that they have been identified and given their own names. There are many different kinds of fallacy. The only way to recognize fallacies is to be aware of their existence, and alert to the temptation of using them.

The 4th-century BCE ancient Greek philosopher Aristotle identified 13 fallacies, including those of "mistaken cause" and "begging the question." The fallacy of mistaken cause arises when one event is wrongly believed to have caused another. For example, it would be wrong to think that night "causes" the Sun to go down. The fallacy of begging the question happens when the premises of an argument assume that the argument's

conclusion is true. An example would be, "My dog is the best dog in the world, because no dog is better than my dog." This argument is begging the question, as all it says is: "My dog is best because my dog is best."

Over the centuries, philosophers have expanded Aristotle's list to include hundreds of fallacies. The most common way to classify these fallacies is by whether they are formal or informal fallacies.

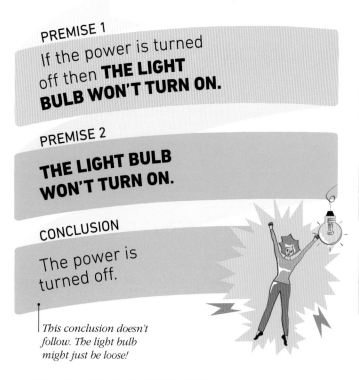

PREMISE 1
If the power is turned off then **THE LIGHT BULB WON'T TURN ON.**

PREMISE 2
THE LIGHT BULB WON'T TURN ON.

CONCLUSION
The power is turned off.

This conclusion doesn't follow. The light bulb might just be loose!

PREMISE 1
If you take a lot of photos, **YOU WILL USE UP THE STORAGE ON YOUR PHONE.**

PREMISE 2
You don't take a lot of photos.

CONCLUSION
YOU WILL NOT USE UP THE STORAGE ON YOUR PHONE.

This conclusion doesn't follow. The storage may be full for other reasons.

▲ **FALLACY OF THE CONVERSE**
If you swap around the terms in a premise, you form the converse of that premise. So the converse of Premise 1 above is, "If the light bulb won't turn on then the power is off." Using this converse to reach the conclusion is a fallacy.

▲ **FALLACY OF THE INVERSE**
The opposite of a statement is called its inverse. The inverse of Premise 1 above is, "If you don't take a lot of photos, you will not use up the storage on your phone." Assuming the inverse of a statement, like in the argument above, creates a fallacy.

FORMAL AND INFORMAL FALLACIES

Some fallacies that are found in deductive arguments (see pp.88–89) are known as formal fallacies. These errors come from the way that an argument has been structured (its form). Two common types of formal fallacy are the fallacy of the converse (see below far left) and the fallacy of the inverse (see below left). Arguments that contain formal fallacies may appear at first glance to be good arguments, but the conclusion is not necessarily true if the premises are true.

Informal fallacies can be found in both deductive and inductive arguments. Informal fallacies are not errors in the structure of an argument, but in the content of the argument itself. There are hundreds of informal fallacies, but a few common examples are given below.

THINK FOR YOURSELF

Imagine that you and your friends have never seen an elephant before. One day, you are all wearing blindfolds, and an elephant stands between you. Reaching out to touch it, what would you say an elephant is like? This question was first asked by Buddhist thinkers. You might say that an elephant is smooth (like its tusk) or that it is thin and hairy (like its tail). Aristotle would call this a fallacy of composition, which mistakes the qualities of part of a thing for the qualities of the thing itself.

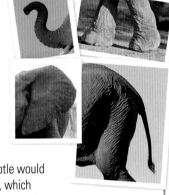

USING FALLACIES
While fallacies are logical errors, they are often used intentionally by those who want to convince people with their arguments, such as politicians or advertisers.

APPEAL TO AUTHORITY
Sometimes people claim the support of an expert who is supposedly an authority in a subject as proof of an argument. But appealing to authority like this doesn't make the argument itself any better.

AD HOMINEM
An *ad hominem* (Latin for "to the person") fallacy attacks a person, rather than their arguments. "You shouldn't believe him, he's a liar" doesn't prove that what someone is saying is false.

STRAW MAN
If a person alters their opponent's arguments to make them easier to defeat, they are said to be "attacking a straw man"—they are not dealing with the real argument.

SLIPPERY SLOPE
"If you go out with your friends, then you won't do your homework and you will fail your exam" is a slippery slope fallacy. It isn't always true that one thing will lead to others.

FALSE DILEMMA
A false dilemma is presented as a limited choice, for example: "You can have a dog, or you can have a cat." If other options are available, this is a false dilemma.

REALLY?

OH, COME ON!

I AGREE.

WHAT?

What is a paradox?

A paradox is a statement or an argument that seems to be based on good reasoning, but that leads to a conclusion that is either contradictory or appears to be ridiculous. A paradox is much more thought-provoking than a fallacy (see pp.90–91), which is just faulty reasoning. It's often difficult to say exactly what is wrong with a paradox.

Paradoxes can show the inconsistencies between how we think and talk about the world, and how the world actually is. Philosophers from many cultures have observed or come up with paradoxes, and some of the most ancient are still discussed today.

ZENO'S PARADOXES

The 5th-century BCE ancient Greek philosopher Parmenides believed that everything is made of a single substance, and that this substance is unchanging (see p.19). His student, Zeno of Elea, attempted to prove this by showing that change, and in particular movement, is not possible. He came up with paradoxes that appeared to show that movement is an illusion.

In the paradox of Achilles and the tortoise, Zeno imagined a race between the mythical Greek warrior Achilles and a tortoise. To make it a fairer race, Achilles allows the tortoise to start further ahead of him. It seems sensible to assume that Achilles would easily win against the naturally slow tortoise. But Zeno argued otherwise, and it's difficult to find a flaw in his argument.

Zeno said that when Achilles reaches the point where the tortoise started, the tortoise has moved on. And each time Achilles catches up to the tortoise's former position, the tortoise is further on the track. The gap between the two racers gets smaller and smaller, but the tortoise is always slightly ahead of Achilles. Zeno concluded that Achilles would never be able to run past the tortoise, as Achilles would have to reach the former position of the tortoise an infinite number of times before he could catch up to it.

A similar paradox created by Zeno focuses on the flight of an arrow through the air. Zeno argued that in any one particular instant of the arrow's flight, the arrow

ACHILLES AND THE TORTOISE

In Zeno's paradox of Achilles and the tortoise, Achilles lets the tortoise start in the lead. But no matter how hard Achilles tries to close the gap between himself and the tortoise, the tortoise is always ahead of him.

Achilles begins the race behind the tortoise.

is not moving. When we observe a flying arrow, we're seeing an infinite number of these instants in which the arrow is motionless. This paradox implies that all objects we think of as moving are actually still, and that what we believe to be movement is an illusion.

Philosophers through the centuries have tried to solve the problems in Zeno's paradoxes. Progress was made in the 1600s with the development of calculus—an advanced type of mathematics that studies the nature of change. Calculus helped to untangle some of the issues contained in Zeno's paradoxes by looking at the nature of infinity. But there is still no universally accepted solution to the problems that Zeno posed.

SELF-REFERENTIAL PARADOXES

A self-referential paradox is a type of paradox in which a contradiction arises from the terms of a statement or argument itself. A famous type of self-referential paradox

▲ THE ARROW PARADOX
At any particular instant, an arrow flying through the air is not moving. If the flight of an arrow is made up of these instances, can it really be said that the arrow is moving?

is known as the liar paradox. One of the simplest examples of this kind of paradox is the statement "This sentence is false." If the sentence is false, as it says, then what it says must be true. But if the sentence is true, then what it says must be a lie. In either case, the statement is shown to be contradictory.

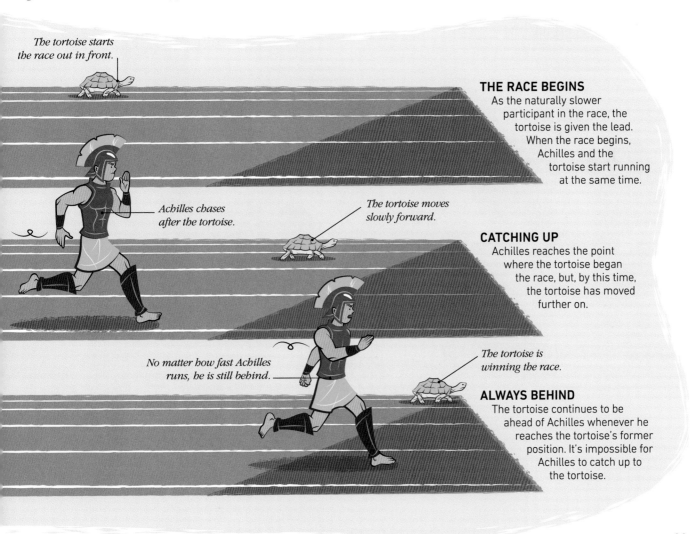

The tortoise starts the race out in front.

Achilles chases after the tortoise.

The tortoise moves slowly forward.

No matter how fast Achilles runs, he is still behind.

The tortoise is winning the race.

THE RACE BEGINS
As the naturally slower participant in the race, the tortoise is given the lead. When the race begins, Achilles and the tortoise start running at the same time.

CATCHING UP
Achilles reaches the point where the tortoise began the race, but, by this time, the tortoise has moved further on.

ALWAYS BEHIND
The tortoise continues to be ahead of Achilles whenever he reaches the tortoise's former position. It's impossible for Achilles to catch up to the tortoise.

The barber paradox, made famous in the 1900s by the British philosopher Bertrand Russell, is another self-referential paradox. The barber paradox asks us to imagine a village in which there is just one barber. The barber is the person "who shaves those, and only those, who do not shave themselves." But if this is the case, then who shaves the barber?

If the barber shaves himself, then according to the statement above he is in the group of people who are not shaved by the barber. So the barber shaves himself and also doesn't shave himself, which is a contradiction. Similarly, if he doesn't shave himself, then he is in the group of people who are shaved by the barber. Again, this leads to a contradiction.

The original Ancient Greek word for a paradox is *parádoxos,* which means "contrary to expectations".

PARADOXES OF LANGUAGE

Some paradoxes arise because of the imprecise meanings of certain words. The ancient puzzle known as the sorites paradox, which dates back to 4th-century BCE Greece, looks at the nature of the word "heap" (the name "sorites" comes from the Greek word *soros,* meaning "heap"). Suppose you had a number of grains of sand in front of you—perhaps a million grains. It would make sense to call this a heap of sand. If you took a grain of sand away, you would still call what is left a heap. If you kept doing this, you'd continue to call it a heap. But this would mean that when you only had three, two, or even one grain in front of you, you could still call it a heap, which seems absurd.

? THE BARBER PARADOX
In the barber paradox, the barber is the person who shaves only those who do not shave themselves. Based on this definition, the barber is faced with the contradiction that he cannot shave himself and must shave himself at the same time.

People who shave themselves

Russell's theory of descriptions solves this problem. According to Russell, definite descriptions (descriptions of unique things, such as "the current king of France") do not get meaning by directly referring to things, but by saying that there is a unique something that fits this description. If there is nothing, or there is more than one thing, that fits the description, then the statement containing the description is false (see below).

GRASS is **GREEN**.

GRASS is **PURPLE**.

??

STEALING is **BAD**.

PICTURING THE WORLD

The Austrian-born philosopher Ludwig Wittgenstein was a student of Russell. During his early career he argued that words had meaning because they picture the world. For Wittgenstein the world is made up of facts. These facts can be either actual facts (things that are true, such as "the grass is green") or possible facts (things that are not true, but that might be true in some possible world, for example "the grass is purple"). Sentences that do not picture an actual or possible fact (such as "that circle is square") are nonsense. This means that ethical statements like "stealing is bad," which do not describe the world, have no meaning. But for Wittgenstein they are not worthless. Rather, they try to say things that can't be put into words.

Wittgenstein would later come to reject his own picture theory of meaning. He instead argued that language is a social activity, and its meaning can be found in how it is used (see pp.100–101).

"THE CURRENT PRESIDENT OF ANTARCTICA IS FREEZING."

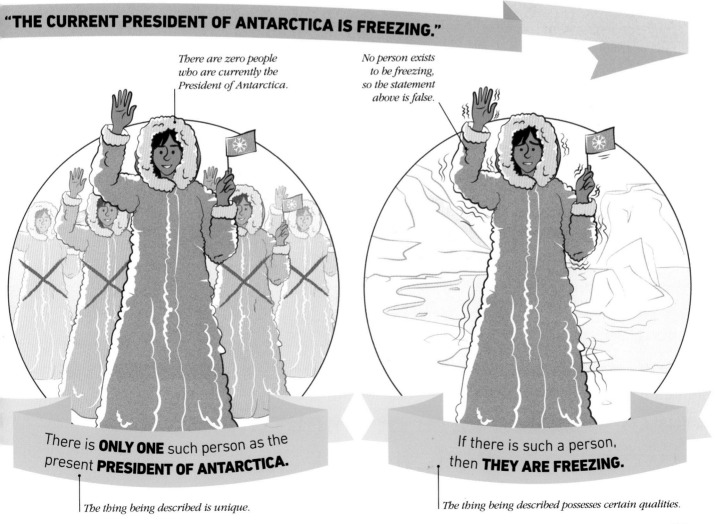

There are zero people who are currently the President of Antarctica.

No person exists to be freezing, so the statement above is false.

There is **ONLY ONE** such person as the present **PRESIDENT OF ANTARCTICA.**

The thing being described is unique.

If there is such a person, then **THEY ARE FREEZING.**

The thing being described possesses certain qualities.

Statements are **meaningful** if they correspond to how things are **pictured in the real world**. Moral statements are therefore meaningless (see pp.96–97).

Meaning is established by **"language games"** based on sets of shared rules. A language referring to the **private inner sensations** of an individual is impossible (see pp.100–101).

Because language is learned through interacting with other language users, I am therefore **not the only person** in the world.

The theory of **family resemblances** describes things which are thought to be linked by **one common factor**, but may only have overlapping **similarities** (see pp.192–193).

Logic **takes care of itself**; all we have to do is to look and see how it does it.

Ludwig Wittgenstein

EXAMINED THE NATURE OF LANGUAGE

Austrian-born Ludwig Wittgenstein spent much of his career in England at Cambridge University. He was notoriously bad-tempered and difficult to work with, but is universally acknowledged as one of the greatest thinkers of the 20th century. His study of the the meaning of words and how we use language transformed the nature of philosophy.

Ludwig Wittgenstein was born in 1889 in Vienna, Austria to a very wealthy family. The youngest of eight intelligent and artistic children, Wittgenstein moved to England in 1908 to study engineering. But he soon became fascinated with the philosophy of mathematics. In 1911 he moved to Cambridge to become a student of Bertrand Russell (see p.96), who was examining the relationship between mathematics, logic, and philosophy. Within a year, Wittgenstein had so impressed his mentor that Russell declared there was nothing more he could teach the young Austrian.

During World War I (1914–1918), Wittgenstein served in the Austrian army. He worked on his philosophy while in the trenches, writing his ideas down in a series of notebooks. These were eventually published in 1921 as the *Tractatus Logico-Philosophicus*. In this book Wittgenstein argued that there are limits to what we can describe in language, and that therefore there are limits to what can be meaningfully said about the world

CINEMA-GOER ▶
Wittgenstein loved American Westerns, and after his lectures he often rushed off to the movie theater, where he sat in the front row eating pork pies.

around us. According to this theory, many philosophical discussions, such as ethical questions about what is "right" and "good," are inherently meaningless.

A CHANGE OF DIRECTION

With this book, Wittgenstein believed that he had solved all the outstanding problems of philosophy, and so he abandoned the subject entirely. He went on to work as a village school teacher, before becoming a gardener.

However, Wittgenstein later came to reject his early philosophical work, and he returned to Cambridge University in 1929, becoming Professor of Philosophy in 1939. There he formulated a new theory about language, which centered on its use as a tool for communication. His new ideas appeared in *Philosophical Investigations* (1953), published two years after his death in 1951.

◀ FIGHTING IN WWI
Wittgenstein fought in Austrian trenches like this one during World War I. He wrote his ideas in notebooks and carried them everywhere in his backpack. During his time in the military, Wittgenstein was awarded several medals for bravery.

How is language used?

Early theories in the philosophy of language were based on the assumption that the meaning of words is linked in some way to the things that they represent in the world (see pp.96–97). In the mid-20th century philosophers of language started to move away from this idea. They began to study how everyday language works in practice, and suggested that the meaning of words can be found in how those words are used.

One of the first philosophers to look at how we actually use language was the 20th-century Austrian-born philosopher Ludwig Wittgenstein. In his early work, Wittgenstein had suggested that language is meaningful if it pictures the world (see p.97). However, he later came to the conclusion that he was mistaken, and that meaning comes from the way we use language.

WORD PLAY ▶
For people who know how to play chess, the word "knight" has a specific meaning. As well as naming the piece itself, it also says something about how the piece moves.

LANGUAGE-GAMES

Wittgenstein realized that language can do so much more than just picturing the world. We can use it to give commands, or to influence people, among many other things. Words are tools that we choose to use depending on the situation. We play what Wittgenstein called language-games—to grasp a word's meaning we must know the rules for the "game" (how it is being used). Even the word "game" itself can relate to numerous

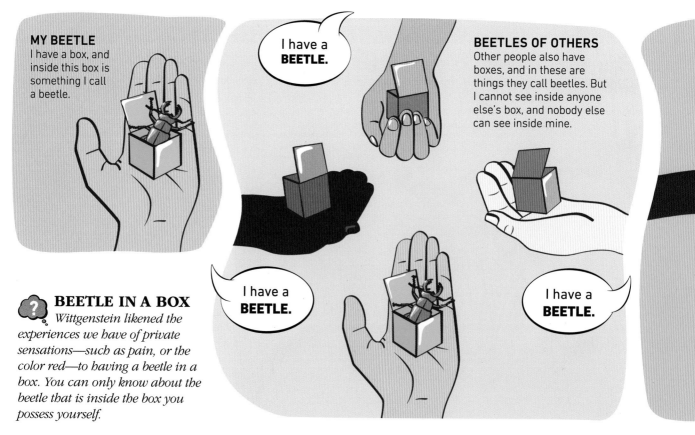

MY BEETLE
I have a box, and inside this box is something I call a beetle.

I have a **BEETLE.**

BEETLES OF OTHERS
Other people also have boxes, and in these are things they call beetles. But I cannot see inside anyone else's box, and nobody else can see inside mine.

I have a **BEETLE.**

I have a **BEETLE.**

? BEETLE IN A BOX
Wittgenstein likened the experiences we have of private sensations—such as pain, or the color red—to having a beetle in a box. You can only know about the beetle that is inside the box you possess yourself.

activities, from sports, to board games, to computer games. The activities that are called games don't have a single thing in common, but they do share some overlapping similarities with each other (for example, sports and board games are often played with other people). Wittgenstein called these similarities "family resemblances" (see pp.191–192). When we are talking about "games," we need to know what the circumstances are to work out which particular language-game we are playing.

PRIVATE LANGUAGE

Wittgenstein said that because the meaning of language is found in its use, there can be no such thing as a private language. By "private" Wittgenstein didn't mean a language we might use in a diary. He meant a language that refers to a person's private sensations. A private language isn't possible because we learn language, and how to use it, from other people in social situations. Language is by its very nature public.

For example, only you yourself know the nature of the experience you have when you feel pain—it's a private sensation that nobody else can feel. You cannot, by pointing to your own experience, teach someone

else what you mean by the word "pain". You can only teach them what you mean by "pain" by describing the experience so that they can relate it to something that they experience. Whether what you experience as pain is the same as what they experience as pain is irrelevant, as there is no way of knowing whether your private sensation is the same as theirs.

Wittgenstein came up with a famous thought experiment about a beetle in a box to help explain these ideas (see below).

Wittgenstein's later ideas about language were only published after his death. They had a lasting impact, not only within philosophy itself but also in many other areas of learning His ideas established the philosophy of language as a branch of thought worthy of study in its own right.

> Wittgenstein suggested that many problems in philosophy arise from misunderstandings about what everyday words actually mean.

A SOCIAL ART

The 20th-century American philosopher Willard Van Orman Quine believed that language is a social art—that its meaning comes from knowing what to say and when to say it. He devised a thought experiment to explain this idea. Imagine that you meet a person who speaks a language that you do not understand. You are with

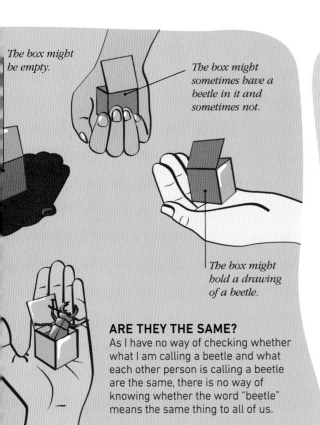

The box might be empty.

The box might sometimes have a beetle in it and sometimes not.

The box might hold a drawing of a beetle.

ARE THEY THE SAME?
As I have no way of checking whether what I am calling a beetle and what each other person is calling a beetle are the same, there is no way of knowing whether the word "beetle" means the same thing to all of us.

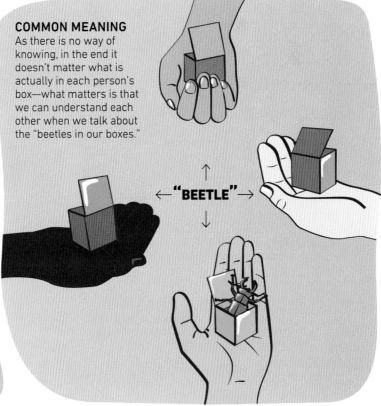

COMMON MEANING
As there is no way of knowing, in the end it doesn't matter what is actually in each person's box—what matters is that we can understand each other when we talk about the "beetles in our boxes."

"BEETLE"

EARS

SPIRIT OF NATURE

BUSH

GAVAGAI!

FAST RUNNER

DINNER

WHAT DOES IT MEAN?
When used by a speaker of an unfamiliar language, the word "gavagai" could mean many things if we have never heard it before. We gain a greater understanding of its meaning the more we hear it in conversation, but we can never be sure we know exactly what it means.

Listeners can have wildly differing thoughts about what new words might mean.

It's difficult to know exactly what is being referred to by the word "gavagai."

this person when a rabbit jumps out of a bush, and the person points and says "gavagai." You might assume that "gavagai" is the word for rabbit—but perhaps they were talking about the bush, or were exclaiming how fast the rabbit moved. As time goes on, more rabbits appear, and you note that every time this happens, your companion says "gavagai." So you conclude that "gavagai" can be reliably translated as "rabbit." Quine insists that this is wrong. "Gavagai" could mean something that you would never be able to discover from how it is used, such as "set of rabbit parts" or "wood-living rabbit."

Even if you decide to learn your companion's language thoroughly, you will still not be able to be certain of the meaning of the word "gavagai," because any other words you learn in the new language to help you understand it will also have the same problem. This suggests that the meaning of words doesn't come from some link between words and things. Instead it comes from the patterns of our behavior, and the way that we participate in language with each other.

SPEECH ACTS

Wittgenstein argued that language had many uses, and the 20th-century English philosopher J.L. Austin took this further. He said that every time we say something we are actually doing something: describing, asking, suggesting, explaining, and so on. He called these

▲ PERFORMING WITH WORDS
According to J.L. Austin, our words don't just describe the world. Every time we talk, we are performing an action. This teacher, by talking to her class, is performing an instructive action. She is not merely speaking, but is doing something with her words.

actions "speech acts." According to Austin, language is something that is performed. When we speak, we want to have some kind of effect on the world. We might want to influence a person, or to teach them, or to make them feel a particular emotion. For Austin words are social tools, and their meanings are the effects we intend them to have on the world.

THE RULES OF CONVERSATION

The 20th-century English thinker Paul Grice said that conversation itself has rules. Children learn these rules first by listening to others' conversations, and then by learning how to converse themselves. There are four rules, which relate to the quality, quantity, relation (relevance), and manner of the conversation. If they are followed, they form a link between what is said and what is understood. Participants in a conversation work cooperatively, both as speakers and as listeners, to make sure they are understood in the way that they intend.

QUALITY (be honest)	Both participants expect the other to tell the truth. They should also only say things for which they have adequate evidence.
QUANTITY (give the correct amount of information)	Participants should be as informative as they can, but not to the extent of giving lots of unnecessary information.
RELATION (be relevant)	A participant should avoid responding with information that has nothing to do with the subject under discussion.
MANNER (be clear)	Participants should strive to be brief, and speak in an organized way. They should also avoid ambiguity and obscure language.

SCIENCE

Philosophers of science don't tackle scientific questions or attempt to make their own discoveries—that's the job of scientists. Instead, they are concerned with questions about the nature of science. For example, they ask about whether science must follow a particular method, how science progresses, and how trustworthy science is. The philosophy of science also examines the social and ethical issues surrounding scientific developments.

Does science have a method?

At the core of science is empirical research. Science is based on the principle that ideas need to be tested, or demonstrated to be true, rather than assuming that ideas are correct. Scientists often make predictions about what they will find, known as hypotheses, and then test these predictions to see if they are in fact true.

Modern science as we know it today did not really begin until the 16th and 17th centuries. But even in the ancient world, thinkers known as natural philosophers made observations about the world and came up with hypotheses to predict events.

NATURAL PHILOSOPHY

The 4th-century BCE ancient Greek philosopher Aristotle was one of the earliest natural philosophers. He made careful observations of the world, collecting enough data to make hypotheses about nature. He described many forms of animal and plant life, organizing them into groups based on their features. Some of these groupings are still used in biology today. But although Aristotle observed nature closely and made predictions based on these observations, he did not carry out experiments to test hypotheses.

In the 10th century, Ibn al-Haytham, a Muslim thinker born in what is now modern-day Iraq, carried out groundbreaking research on the nature of vision. Many

EARLY EXPERIMENTS
Ibn al-Haytham's experiments gave us a greater understanding of light. In his pinhole camera, light passed through a small hole in straight lines. This resulted in an inverted reflection, cast on the opposite wall.

> # I **open** and lay out **a new** and certain **path** for the **mind to proceed** in.
>
> **FRANCIS BACON**, *Novum Organum* (1620)

of his contemporaries thought that the eyes emitted light. But Ibn al-Haytham used experiments to prove that they were wrong, and that light instead enters the eye. Ibn al-Haytham was never satisfied with untested ideas. He thought that we have a duty to question anything that we learn, and that experimentation is an essential tool that allows us to find evidence that either supports or contradicts our theories. These principles became a key part of scientific research, and remain hugely important in how science is practiced today.

TOWARD A SCIENTIFIC METHOD

In his book *Novum Organum*, published in 1620, the English philosopher Francis Bacon put forward his ideas on the best way to research scientific knowledge about the world. He wanted to base scientific knowledge on empirical evidence, and set out a method that made use of induction. This method relied on making hypotheses from generalizations based on a set of observations (see right). However, Bacon believed that generalizations needed to be

OBSERVATION
Make careful observations, organizing and examining them closely to produce facts of good quality.

HYPOTHESIS
Generalize from observations to create or modify a hypothesis—a starting point for further investigation.

EXPERIMENTATION
Test the hypothesis by designing and performing experiments that will provide further data for observation.

▲ BACONIAN METHOD
Bacon's scientific method relies on three main stages: observation, hypothesis, and experimentation. Further observations are made from the data that experiments provide, and the cycle repeats. So scientific knowledge continually builds from what has gone before.

consistent with observations. They should never go beyond the available evidence into guesswork. Bacon was also interested in finding the causes of scientific results. He tested them under a range of different circumstances to identify the likeliest cause of any result and to eliminate alternative explanations.

Bacon's techniques have since come to be known as the Baconian method. They were a key part of the Scientific Revolution that swept across Europe in the 16th and 17th centuries, leading to an astounding number of new scientific discoveries and inventions. They also formed the basis of scientific methodology right up until the present day. Over the centuries, scientists have expanded Bacon's ideas, bringing in extra stages, such as peer review—a process in which a scientist's findings are reviewed by other scientists who work in the same field to check their results.

In the second half of the 20th century, however, some philosophers began to question whether scientists really do always follow a method that is based on these ideas, or even if they follow a method at all. Some of these philosophers have suggested that the progress of science might not be so simple (see pp.112–115).

FRANCIS BACON

The English politician and philosopher Francis Bacon (1561–1626) served as First Lord Chancellor to Britain's King James I. His lasting reputation, though, is based on the ideas about scientific method that he set out in *Novum Organum* (1620). Bacon died from pneumonia, which he is thought to have caught while performing an experiment on the effect of freezing a chicken by stuffing it with snow.

Are scientific laws facts?

Scientific research has provided us with many laws that appear to explain how the Universe around us works. These laws are generally accepted as true, because they successfully predict outcomes. For example, we know that if we drop a ball it will fall to the ground, because that's how the law of gravity works. But some philosophers have argued that we have no real basis for believing that these scientific laws are actually facts.

Science can only be based on available evidence, but we don't have evidence about everything in the Universe. For example, we don't have evidence of future events. This means that scientists must use a type of reasoning known as induction to create, test, and assess scientific theories and laws. Inductive reasoning uses observations of particular instances that have happened in the past to support general conclusions. For instance, if a person lives in a place where the Sun has risen every morning of every day in known history, then it could be considered safe to expect that the Sun will rise in that place tomorrow, and every day after that.

THE PROBLEM OF INDUCTION

The 18th-century Scottish philosopher David Hume saw a problem with inductive reasoning in science. Induction relies on assumptions that everything in nature follows an unchanging pattern, and that the future will resemble the past. But according to Hume, there can be no arguments to prove that "those instances of which we have had no experience, resemble those of which we have." Just because the Sun has always risen in the past, that doesn't necessarily mean that the Sun will rise tomorrow. Hume suggested that science is a matter of custom and habit. We cannot help believing that the Sun will rise tomorrow, because it always has.

Yesterday   **Today**   **Tomorrow**

◀ WILL THE SUN RISE TOMORROW?
No matter how many examples from the past we can find of the Sun rising, these past examples can't guarantee that the Sun will rise again tomorrow.

ALL SWANS ARE WHITE

Up until the end of the 1600s, Europeans believed the statement "all swans are white" to be true. But this claim was falsified when Dutch traders brought back news of black swans in Australia in 1697.

The discovery of just a single black swan **falsifies** the theory that "all swans are white," and a **new scientific theory** must be formulated to take its place.

According to Popper, the theory that **"all swans are white"** is scientific because it is **falsifiable**—it is possible for it to be proven false.

FALSIFICATION THEORY

For more than a century, the problem of induction raised doubts about how far we can trust the theories of science. But in the 1900s, the Austrian-born philosopher Karl Popper suggested a different way of looking at the problem. He argued that although no amount of experimentation or observation can prove a scientific law to be true, it only takes a single negative result to show it to be false. Popper said that as scientists cannot prove their theory to be correct, they should instead create experiments that attempt to "falsify," or disprove, their claims. If a scientific theory survives persistent attempts at falsification, then it deserves to be considered a law. But this law will only be in effect for as long as it remains unfalsified.

Popper saw falsification as central to scientific progress. Science advances when a theory is shown to be false, and scientists must come up with a better explanation to take its place. He strongly believed that claims must be falsifiable in order to count as science. If there is no way that a theory can possibly be proven false, then it has no place in science. Popper rejected the claims to science of astrology and psychology—calling them "pseudo-science"—because he believed that the claims they made were not falsifiable.

KARL POPPER

Karl Popper (1902–1994) was born in Austria, but due to his Jewish heritage, he sought refuge from Nazi persecution by accepting a teaching post in New Zealand in 1938. He eventually moved to England in 1946 where he remained until his death. Popper wrote on many areas of philosophy, but is particularly known for his contribution to the philosophy of science. His theory of falsification. helped to establish the study of science as a branch of philosophy.

David Hume

THE GREAT EMPIRICAL SKEPTIC

The Scottish thinker David Hume claimed that knowledge comes solely from experience (a point of view known as empiricism), and that because of this we can know nothing for sure (a point of view known as skepticism). He is best known for his scientific approach to the study of human nature.

SCIENCE

David Hume was born in 1711 in Edinburgh, Scotland. His father died when he was three years old, and his mother brought him up on her own. From an early age, Hume had a great interest in literature, history, and philosophy. He attended the University of Edinburgh to study law, but he left before graduating because he did not think that his teachers had anything left to teach him. He spent several years in France, developing ideas about a "new science of thought." He studied so intensely that he became quite sick.

A SERIES OF REJECTIONS

In his first book, *A Treatise of Human Nature* (1739), Hume argued that passion, not reason, governs human behavior. He also suggested that our belief in cause and effect—that one thing can be seen to cause another thing—cannot be justified by reason.

Hume expected the *Treatise* to be a great success. To his disappointment, it was heavily criticized. Seeing the book as a failure, he decided to develop his ideas further. This resulted in two more important works: *An Enquiry Concerning Human Understanding* (1748), and *An Enquiry Concerning the Principles of Morals* (1751). However, these were also poorly received at the time.

Hume applied for a senior position at the University of Edinburgh, but was rejected because his books questioned the existence of God. He became a librarian, and wrote *History of England* (1754), which received much greater acclaim than his books of philosophy.

Hume lived a quiet life, though he had many good friends and was well respected. He was regarded as a major philosopher only after his death in 1776. His works later influenced the philosopher Immanuel Kant (see pp.62–63), and the scientist Albert Einstein.

All **knowledge** comes from two types of **experience**: **outward impressions** gained through our five senses, and **inward impressions** through reflecting on past experience.

Predicting what will happen in the future based on what has happened in the past can lead to **unreliable conclusions** (see p.108).

Humans are **ruled by passions**, but **reason is "instrumental."** We use it to pursue our goals and desires (see p.134).

Statements can be divided into those that are about **relations of ideas** and those that are about **matters of fact** in the real world. Anything else is meaningless (see pp.86–87).

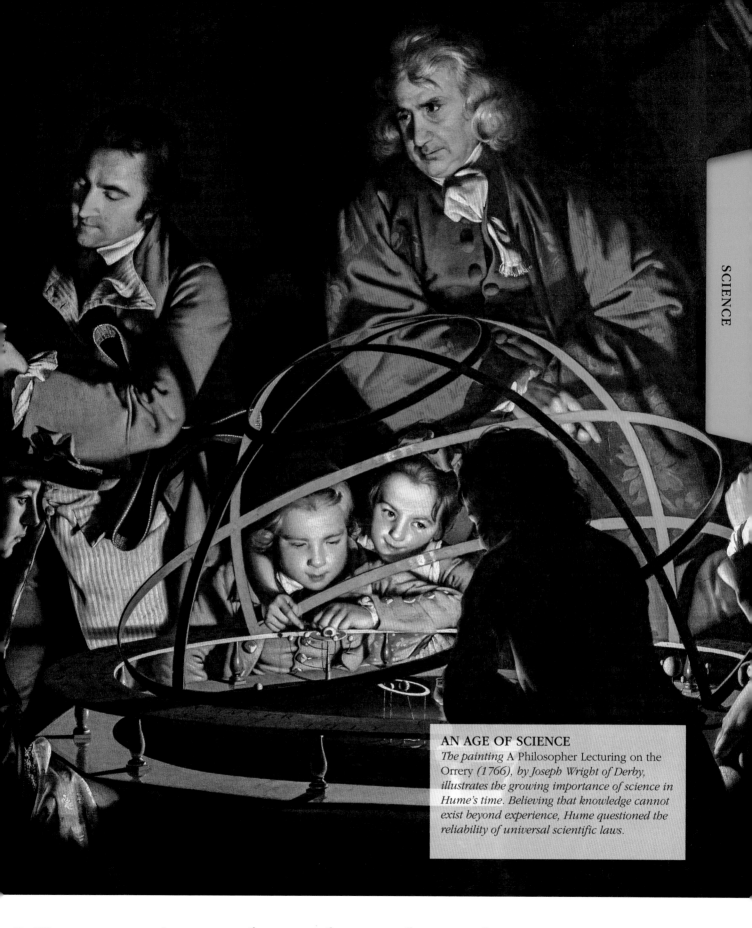

AN AGE OF SCIENCE
The painting A Philosopher Lecturing on the
Orrery *(1766), by Joseph Wright of Derby,
illustrates the growing importance of science in
Hume's time. Believing that knowledge cannot
exist beyond experience, Hume questioned the
reliability of universal scientific laws.*

Reason is, and ought only to be,
the **slave of the passions**.

How does science progress?

The science of a few hundred years ago bears little resemblance to the science of today. Science is continually making progress, with new discoveries leading to new technologies, which in turn make researching further discoveries easier. In the late 1900s, philosophers of science began to seriously investigate how scientific progress actually works, and many new theories began to emerge.

The scientific method laid out by the 16th-century English philosopher Francis Bacon (see p.107) suggests that science progresses gradually and continuously. New hypotheses are theorized and tested, and are then added to the collected store of scientific knowledge. According to the Austrian-born 20th-century philosopher Karl Popper, when some of these theories are shown to be false, they must be replaced by new theories, progressing science further (see p.109).

NO FIRM FOUNDATION

One problem with the traditional view of science is that new hypotheses are built on earlier hypotheses, which must be assumed to be correct. The 20th-century Austrian-born philosopher Otto Neurath

Like sailors who must make sure their **boat doesn't sink**, scientists must replace theories without disturbing the **foundations of science**.

The boat can **spring a new leak** at any time, just as scientific theories always have the **potential to be proven false**.

> Likened science to a boat which... we must rebuild plank by plank while staying afloat in it.
> **WILLARD VAN ORMAN QUINE**, *Word and Object* (1960)

compared the progress of science (and many other branches of knowledge) to a boat in need of repair in the middle of an ocean. You can replace small parts of the boat, but not the entire hull, or the boat will sink. In a similar way, when scientists discard a scientific theory that has proven to be false, the alternative theory that replaces it has to be built upon the same scientific foundations as the incorrect theory. If these foundations prove to be false as well, then any theories based upon them may turn out not to br true.

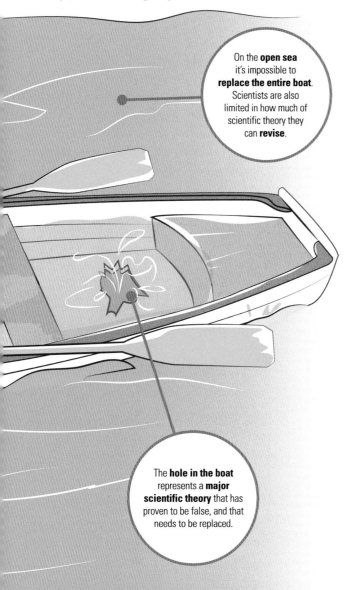

Quine considered philosophy to be a part of science, and believed that philosophical knowledge must be treated in the same way as scientific knowledge.

NEURATH'S BOAT

The analogy of Neurath's boat compares scientists to sailors who must make repairs to their boat while they are at sea. Scientists can replace bits of scientific knowledge, but must keep its foundations intact.

On the **open sea** it's impossible to **replace the entire boat**. Scientists are also limited in how much of scientific theory they can **revise**.

The **hole in the boat** represents a **major scientific theory** that has proven to be false, and that needs to be replaced.

THE WEB OF BELIEF

The analogy of Neurath's boat was popularized by the 20th-century American philosopher Willard Van Orman Quine, who also had his own ideas on scientific progress. For Quine, science is part of an interconnected "web of belief" that encompasses the whole of human knowledge. Scientific statements are related to numerous other statements that make up this web of knowledge. Before we can assess scientific theories and analyze whether or not they should be accepted as scientific knowledge, we must look at their contribution to the interconnected web of belief as a whole.

BACKGROUND ASSUMPTIONS

Another philosopher who was interested in how scientific progress fits into an overall framework of knowledge was the 20th-century French philosopher Michel Foucault. He took the view that science happens within a particular historical "field of knowledge" that he called an "episteme." Scientists are unconsciously influenced by the episteme in which they work, and take its underlying assumptions for granted.

In his book *The Order of Things* (1966), Foucault outlined the features of historical epistemes. He noted that the episteme of late medieval Europe (from around 1250 until 1500) assumed that the Universe was ordered and interconnected. Everything was the way it was for a reason. An important concept in this episteme was that of "resemblance." It was believed that when things appear to resemble each other, they do so for a reason. For example, the appearance of herbs and plants was believed to give clues to their medicinal uses.

TOOTHWORT ▶
In the episteme of medieval Europe, the plant Lathraea (commonly known as toothwort) was believed to be a cure for toothache because its flowers resembled rows of teeth. Modern science has dismissed this claim.

ARISTOTLE
Aristotle argued that objects fall to the ground because they are attracted to the center of the Earth. Objects fall at different speeds according to their mass.

Crisis

Normal science

GALILEO GALILEI
Galileo demonstrated that objects with different masses fall at the same speed, contradicting Aristotle's theory.

THE THEORY OF GRAVITY

Using Kuhn's model of periods of normal science followed by periods of crises, it's possible to examine the scientific revolutions of thought that occurred in the history of the theory of gravity, from Aristotle to Albert Einstein.

This episteme began to fall apart during the Scientific Revolution in the 16th and 17th centuries, when testing and experimentation replaced resemblance as the basis for claims to scientific knowledge.

PARADIGM SHIFTS

Perhaps the most influential theory about the progress of science was laid out by the 20th-century American philosopher Thomas Kuhn in his book *The Structure of Scientific Revolutions* (1962). Like Foucault, Kuhn suggested that science takes place within a particular historical background, but he had a very different idea about the nature of this background.

Kuhn said that at any particular point in time, there is a view of the world that scientists have agreed on. He called this a "paradigm." While scientists are still in agreement on this paradigm, we are in a period of what Kuhn called "normal science." During normal science, the key theories and assumptions of the current paradigm remain intact. But over time, anomalies begin to appear as scientists make observations that don't fit in with these theories and assumptions. If enough of these anomalies gather, science reaches a crisis point and the paradigm may "shift" to account for these anomalies,

creating a scientific revolution. This revolution produces a new paradigm that eventually settles down to become the new basis for a period of normal science.

According to Kuhn, the progress of science alternates between these periods of normal science and crisis. This process can be seen in the development of the theory of gravity within the study of physics (see above). In Kuhn's model of progress, scientific theories are not immediately overturned as soon as observations

Scientist   **Palm reader**

▲ ALTERNATIVES TO SCIENCE

Feyerabend argued that science has no justification for dismissing alternative traditions such as palmistry or acupuncture as "non-scientific." Science itself is not inherently better than these traditions, and so cannot be the standard against which they are judged.

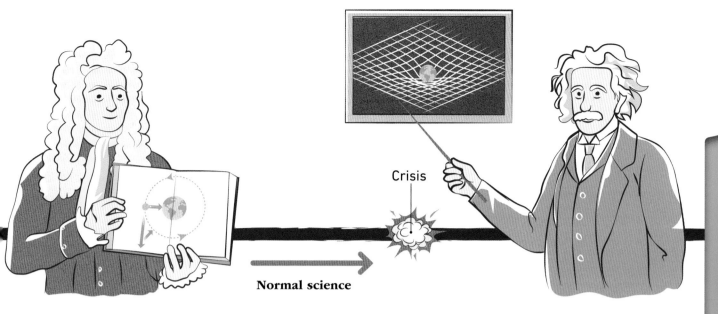

SIR ISAAC NEWTON
Newton discovered that gravity is a force, and that it is this force that explain's the Moon's orbit around the Earth.

Normal science

Crisis

ALBERT EINSTEIN
Einstein discovered that very large objects such as planets can distort the gravitational fields around them.

begin to suggest that they are wrong. Kuhn argues that science doesn't work that way in practice—scientific communities may hold on to theories and beliefs for some time, despite evidence that seems to show they are incorrect. For example, many scientists continued to believe that the Earth lay at the center of the Universe, even when astronomical observations were accumulating to show that this wasn't the case. It takes a revolution to overturn one paradigm and replace it with another. This seems to go against the philosopher Karl Popper's idea that once a theory is shown to be false, it is replaced by something better (see p.109).

ANYTHING GOES

The 20th-century Austrian-born philosopher Paul Feyerabend argued that the development of science doesn't follow as strict a pattern as the one suggested by Kuhn. He said that when a scientific revolution occurs, the scientific assumptions that are part of the old way of thinking no longer have any relevance. This means that a new theory based on previous science is no better than a theory that doesn't take previous scientific assumptions into account at all.

Feyerabend believed that science is full of accidents and guesswork. It doesn't progress according to any rules, and if the philosophy of science demands such rules, it will limit scientific progress. According to Feyerabend, there is no such thing as "scientific method." If we look at how science has developed and progressed in practice, the only "method" that we can see is that "anything goes."

MARY MIDGLEY

Born in London, the English philosopher Mary Midgley (1919–2018) was known for her work in the areas of science, ethics, animal rights, and conservation. In her writings on the philosophy of science, she argued that myths and stories play a significant part in scientific progress For instance, the 17th-century idea that human beings are comparable to machines still has influence on science today.

Feyerabend argued that because a scientific method doesn't exist, science doesn't really deserve the great status that it is given in Western society. Feyerabend was particularly critical of scientists who expressed negative opinions about different traditions, such as astrology or alternative medicine. He felt that such opinions showed how scientists can often see science as superior to other ways of thinking about the world, when in fact it is no better. Alternative traditions outside of science cannot be judged on scientific grounds, and should not be so easily dismissed by modern scientists.

Is science objective?

Science has a reputation for being more objective than other methods of studying the world. It is generally believed to be concerned with facts, unaffected by human biases or ethical values. But philosophers of science question this view, saying that science is always conducted from a certain perspective.

While it's usually thought that science should be as objective as possible, it's often argued that it is difficult to disentangle science from the society in which it takes place. The time and place in which scientists live can drive science in a particular direction. For example, during World War I (1914–1918) and World War II (1939–1945), many scientists took part in research that had military applications, eventually leading to the discovery of nuclear energy.

FACTS ABOUT THE WORLD

Whatever the goals of scientific research, can scientific data be considered objective? Many believe the task of scientists is to uncover facts that exist in the world. While two people might disagree on whether the performance of a piece of music is too loud, a scientific measurement in decibels provides an "absolute" fact about the world. But the contemporary British sociologist of science Harry Collins argued that these facts are not absolute. Scales of measurement are set up by scientists, and experiment results are interpreted by scientists—and scientists have their own biases.

DIFFERENT PERSPECTIVES

The contemporary American philosopher Donna Haraway said that science is traditionally understood to have a "gaze from nowhere," meaning that it doesn't come from any particular perspective. But Haraway argued that all knowledge is human knowledge, so it therefore has a human perspective.

Feminist philosophers argue that the dominant perspective in many fields of knowledge is that of white males. Feminist standpoint theory suggests that groups that are marginalized by society, whether on the basis

TOO HOT

TOO COLD

64°F

18°C

OBJECTIVE FACTS ▶
A person from a cool climate may think that a particular day is hot, while a person from a warm climate might think it cold, even though it is the same temperature. A scientific measurement of temperature in degrees offers a more objective fact about the world than people's opinions.

Unlike a perspective, which is taken for granted, a standpoint is created collectively by a marginalized group, such as women.

HAVING A STANDPOINT

According to feminist standpoint theory, marginalized groups have a "knowledge advantage" because their standpoint allows them to see the dominant perspective from both the outside and within.

Race and gender are not the only standpoints that can be valuable to science.

Any marginalized group, such as people of color, can achieve a standpoint through political struggle.

The dominant perspective holds the traditional view of science.

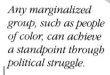

of gender, race, able-bodiedness, and so on, have a particular standpoint (a collective identity). This standpoint enables them to view science with a more critical eye than the dominant perspective, because they exist outside of it. Feminist standpoint theorists argue that the views and opinions of the marginalized are valuable to science, because they can see the problems within it more clearly.

The contemporary philosopher Helen Longino agreed that access to many different opinions is useful for science. She argued that theories only become scientific knowledge when they are criticized from a number of different perspectives. The more diverse these perspectives are in terms of their beliefs and values, the more objective that scientific knowledge becomes.

The Nuremberg Code is a set of ethical principles created in 1947 that lays out guidelines for scientific testing on human subjects.

ETHICAL STANDARDS

One way that scientists have attempted to increase the objectivity of science is to create ethical standards that guide how scientific knowledge should be researched. These standards help science to progress by ensuring that scientific research is both reliable and consistent across the world. Most of the principles expressed in these standards relate to reducing levels of bias in scientific research. For instance, they stress the importance of honesty in reporting data, openly sharing experimental methods among scientists, and replicating experiments to confirm results. But some standards look at moral obligations that science has to society. The rights of humans and animals involved in scientific experimentation is a particular area of concern.

Mary Warnock

REDEFINED ETHICAL BOUNDARIES FOR EDUCATION AND SCIENCE

English philosopher Mary Warnock was interested in ethical debates about subjects such as education and medical science. She is remembered for her contribution to two influential reports. The first was about children with special education needs, which led to a more inclusive education system in Britain. The second discussed the ethics of using human embryos for infertility treatments and medical research.

Born Helen Mary Wilson in 1924 in Winchester, England, Warnock was the youngest of seven children. Her father died seven months before she was born, and she was raised by her mother and a nanny. She studied Classics at school and went to Oxford University, although her studies were interrupted by World War II. In 1949 she married British philosopher Geoffrey Warnock and they had five children. Warnock lectured at the university, and later became the principal at Oxford High School for Girls.

ETHICS IN ACTION

Warnock was interested in the practical application of ethics, especially in the field of biological research (this is known as bioethics). This interest led her to take on a number of roles on committees that addressed the biggest moral issues of the day (including the education of children with special needs, environmental pollution, animal experimentation, and human fertilization).

Her work on these committees led to the publication of two "Warnock Reports"—the first in 1978 and the second in 1984. The 1978 report argued for children with special education needs to be taught alongside other children in mainstream schools—at this time in Britain, such children were normally educated separately. The 1984 report investigated the ethical issues surrounding the use of human embryos in infertility treatments and medical research. It found that because an embryo cannot feel pain before it is 14 days old (before this, its spinal cord and nervous system has not yet developed), there should be a 14-day limit on human embryo experimentation. The report led to changes in British law, and also provided a blueprint for laws on the use of embryos in scientific research in many other countries around the world.

Warnock died in 2019, aged 94. As a philosopher, she bridged the gap between theory and practice, and made lasting contributions to both education and science.

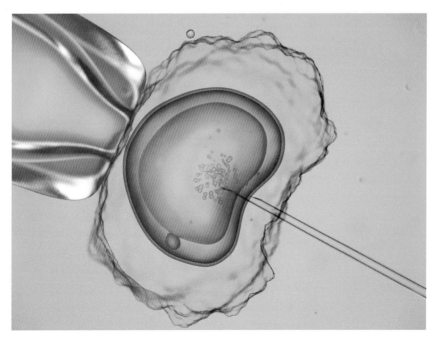

◀ ARTIFICIAL FERTILIZATION
Warnock chaired a committee to discuss the ethics of in vitro fertilization (a type of fertilization in which an egg and a sperm are combined outside of a female's body) and experimentation on human embryos.

Morality should **not be based** on **religion,** but is something to be debated.

Children with **special educational needs** should be taught in **mainstream schools,** not separate institutions.

Women should have the **right** to make **informed choices** over whether or not to have babies.

We must **learn morality** from **each other,** not God.

RIGHT AND WRONG

In philosophy, the study of what is right and wrong is known as ethics. It explores how we decide what is "good" and "bad," and whether these values ever change. Philosophers have discussed the kind of life people should aim to live, and whether we can make changes to improve the world around us. They have also examined if people are truly free to decide upon their own actions.

What is a good life?

In the ancient world, Greek and Chinese philosophers thought that the most important ethical question had to do with what it takes to lead a "good" life. They tried to determine whether this means a life of virtue, and whether virtuous living is the same as a life of pleasure. Philosophers of ethics have explored what kind of people we should *be*, and what we should *do* to live a good life.

For some philosophers, a good life is a life of virtue. This is known as "virtue ethics." In China, during the 6th century BCE, Confucius argued for a form of virtue ethics and explained how role models (*junzi*) provide examples on how to lead a good life. According to him, the aim of a good life is to cultivate virtue. Among the Confucian virtues are *ren* (kindness), *yi* (justice), and *li* (appropriate behavior, e.g. greeting your parents and teachers). They are symbolic ways of expressing respect for others.

According to Confucian ethics, we are part of a large network of ethical relationships, which includes the people we interact with on a regular basis. This means we have responsibilities toward our parents, carers, and teachers, just as they have responsibilities to us.

EVERYTHING IN MODERATION

Aristotle, a 4th-century BCE ancient Greek philosopher, also based his ethics on virtue. In his view, the goal of life is to achieve happiness. He described happiness as the ongoing task of working toward becoming the best people we can be. Just as most people can physically train their bodies through exercise, they can also train themselves to be happy by developing their virtues.

Aristotle believed that moderation is the path to virtue. His Theory of the Mean said that we must find a middle ground between the two extremes of any situation (see illustration, right). Every virtue has an excess (too much) and a deficiency (too little). So, for the virtue of courage, there is rashness (an excess of courage) and cowardice (a deficiency of courage). Virtuous behavior is achieved by maintaining a balance between the two.

PEACE OF MIND

In the 3rd century BCE, another ancient Greek philosopher, Epicurus, stated that a good life is one that is free from physical pain and mental anxiety—part of the philosophical tradition of hedonism, where pleasure is the goal of a good life. He thought that philosophy had a therapeutic job: it could treat or cure the soul of unnecessary desires. According to Epicurus, most pleasurable experiences are not as we expect them to

THE GARDEN

In c.200 BCE, the ancient Greek philosopher Epicurus bought a house outside Athens and made a place to teach outside in its grounds. This became known as "The Garden." The school was a place where the students could live simply with each other. Epicurus and his followers welcomed everyone, including women and enslaved people, which was unusual for the time. They promoted a life of moderation in order to achieve peace of mind—their ultimate aim for a good life.

DEFICIENCY

This singer is very nervous and singing too quietly for the judges to hear him. In Aristotle's terms, his performance is deficient.

EXCESS

By singing too loudly, this singer is making the judges uncomfortable. According to Aristotle's doctrine, her performance is excessive.

THE MEAN

This performer is singing neither too softly nor too loudly. Her performance is perfectly balanced, allowing the judges to award her maximum points. According to Aristotle, this is the mean, on which all behavior should be based.

THE THEORY OF THE MEAN

Aristotle recommended moderation when trying to live a good life. In this singing competition, the judges do not reward the quiet and loud singers, preferring the happy medium offered by the final contestant.

be: they vanish too quickly and they always leave us wanting more. In Epicurus's hedonism, pleasure given by peace of mind is a better and a more lasting state.

WHAT REALLY MATTERS

In the 1900s, American philosopher Robert Nozick provided an interesting response to the ancient Greek philosophy of hedonism. In his thought experiment known as The Experience Machine, he described an isolation tank whereby a person could be plugged into a device that gave them the chance to immerse in nothing but pleasurable experiences. These experiences could be selected to suit each person, and would be indistinguishable from life outside of the machine. Nozick felt that most people would still choose real life over the machine, revealing that there is value in having your own experiences, even at the cost of not having infinite pleasure.

BEING AUTHENTIC

Zhuangzi is both the name of a Chinese philosopher from the 4th century BCE and also the name of a book on Daoism attributed to him. Zhuangzi the philosopher encouraged people to be authentic (true to themselves), and to live a simple life that honors the flow of nature. One way to do this is by what Zhuangzi called *wuwei*

("nonaction") the skill of letting nature take its course. This does not mean doing nothing, but acting with a spontaneous, unforced skilfulness. One example that Zhuangi gives is of a cook's mastery over their art in the kitchen, when they are totally absorbed in their work.

IN HARMONY WITH NATURE

Other philosophers also focused on living in harmony with nature as the means of achieving a good life. The cynics were a group of 5th-century BCE ancient Greek thinkers who rejected the conventional ways of living of the time. They proposed living a simple life that was close to the most natural state of humans. One of the most famous cynics, Diogenes, was renowned for living a life of poverty on the streets of Athens. It is said that when Alexander the Great walked toward him, Diogenes told the emperor to get out of his way, as he was blocking the sunlight. This legendary story illustrates how a good life is about attending to our natural needs, rather than worrying about power, authority, or fame.

HIPPARCHIA OF MARONEIA

Hipparchia (c.355/370–415 CE) was a cynic philosopher from ancient Greece, as well as a talented astronomer and mathematician. She was also a gifted teacher, and in her philosophy rejected materialism (see pp.24–25). Hipparchia frequently challenged the role of women in society in her impressive public speeches, and she was seen as unconventional. Cynics were against marriage, but by choosing to marry fellow cynic philosopher Crates, she and her husband defied the customs of even their own philosophical beliefs.

The guests don't understand why their friend doesn't want their company.

His friends try to attract his attention.

> # Perhaps what we **desire** is to live in **contact with reality**
> **ROBERT NOZICK**, *Anarchy, State and Utopia* (1974)

EVERYDAY ETHICS

Stoicism was a branch of ancient Greek philosophy, dating from the 3rd century BCE, that valued wisdom and self-discipline. It stated that people must train themselves to be immune to misfortune, and to endure everyday life without complaint. They should also be free to follow what they believe is right because it keeps them in harmony with their true nature. The Stoics claimed that people are good by nature and they are initially drawn to what is appropriate for their survival, such as food and warmth, and not necessarily what is pleasurable. As they mature people develop their search for what they believe is virtuous. The Roman emperor Marcus Aurelius was a stoic, who said that it was better for people to practice their values than to preach them.

▲ DIOGENES AND ALEXANDER
Diogenes chose a simple lifestyle, which included sleeping in a barrel. He even rejected help from Alexander the Great, asking only that he step aside to allow his basic need for sunlight.

The virtual party is fun, but the boy could have a good time with his real friends, too.

The party features virtual friends and only positive experiences.

THE VIRTUAL EXPERIENCE
In our version of The Experience Machine, a boy is enjoying a virtual party, while his friends are waiting outside for a real one. Which experience would you choose: the perfect celebration with virtual friends, or a real party with your actual friends?

FOLLOWING THE PATH
From its origins in northern India, Buddhism spread quickly throughout East and Southeast Asia. These modern-day Buddhist monks in Bangkok, Thailand, practice meditation to clear their minds of distractions, and to focus on the path to enlightenment.

I teach **one thing** and one thing only: **suffering** and the **end of suffering**.

Siddhārtha Gautama

FOUNDER OF BUDDHISM

Siddhārtha Gautama, also known as the Buddha, was a South Asian philosopher and spiritual teacher. Much of his life is shrouded in legend. His beliefs and teachings lie at the heart of Buddhism, a religion that has become one of the most widely practiced faiths in the world.

According to Buddhist tradition, Siddhārtha Gautama was born into a royal household in c.563 BCE in modern-day Nepal. He spent his childhood living in a palace, unaware of the hardships faced by regular people. One day, while traveling, Siddhārtha saw three things: an old man, a diseased person, and a corpse being cremated. For the first time, he became aware that there was old age, sickness, and death in the world. Moved by the suffering he saw, Siddhārtha realized that there was more to happiness than just physical comforts.

BECOMING THE BUDDHA

Buddhist legend says that at the age of 29 Siddhārtha decided to give up all his possessions and to leave the palace and his family to become an ascetic (a penniless wanderer). He began a quest to solve the problem of human suffering. He deprived himself of basic comforts, hoping that this would free his mind from the desires of his body, which he saw as the cause of his suffering.

One day, Siddhārtha sat down to meditate under a sacred fig tree in northern India—now known as the Bodhi tree—for seven weeks. Here he achieved *nirvana* (enlightenment) and all his desires and suffering disappeared. This is why he is known as the Buddha, which means "awakened one." He then dedicated the rest of his life to teaching his philosophy.

Buddha taught that there are "three marks" of existence. The first is *annicā* (impermanence)—all physical and mental things come into being, and then decay. The second is *duhkha* (unsatisfactoriness)—physical and mental suffering is a natural part of human existence. The last is *anatta* (non-self)—there is no permanent self or soul within human beings. These teachings became the founding principles of Buddhism.

The Buddha died at the age of 80. When he died, he broke free from the cycle of death and rebirth that, according to Buddhist belief, is a human's fate if they do not achieve enlightenment.

The **"Four Noble Truths"** explain what suffering is and how to end it (see pp.154–155).

A person's life should be **equally balanced** between deprivation and indulgence, achieving the **"Middle Way"**.

Negative traits, such as greed and hate, are a **destructive fire**. The only way to get rid of them is to achieve **enlightenment** (see pp.154–155).

Meditation, which involves **emptying the mind** of distracting thoughts, brings peace and focus.

What is a good act?

Most of us would say we know the difference between right and wrong. We may have learned this from our family, our religion, our traditions, or from the laws of society. However, philosophers aren't satisfied with relying on tradition for answers. Instead, they prefer to ask whether there is something about an act that makes us call it "good" or "bad."

There are two different ways of answering the question of what makes a good (or moral) act. One approach is to say that an act is good when it's done for the right reasons, regardless of what happens because of that act. This position is known as deontology. Another approach is to say that a good act is one that brings about the best consequences—the intention of the person is irrelevant. This is called consequentialism.

The *Bhagavad Gita* is an ancient text of Hindu philosophy that teaches the importance of intention and *dharma*, a concept of morality that includes duty. It tells the story of Prince Arjuna and his charioteer and teacher, the god Krishna. As he is about to enter battle, Arjuna is troubled by the death and destruction it will bring. Krishna advises the prince to fight, because it is his duty as a warrior. The consequences of the battle—good and bad—are out of his control.

THE SAME RULE FOR EVERYONE
The idea of duty also features in the philosophy of the 18th-century German thinker Immanuel Kant. He thought that when people find themselves unable to make a decision, they should ask, "What is my duty?" Doing your duty can be hard, as it might go against what you naturally want and feel. For example, you know you *should* finish your homework, even if it's not what you *feel* like doing.

Kant thought that our moral behavior should be guided by reason, not emotions. To help us decide how best to do the right thing, Kant gave us a tool called the "Categorical Imperative." Imagine a situation in which you're tempted to tell a "white lie" to a friend to avoid hurting their feelings. You should first ask yourself, "What would happen if everyone told white lies?" Clearly, we wouldn't want a world where everybody lied. So, for Kant, telling the truth is a categorical (non-negotiable) imperative (something that must be done). Telling the truth becomes what he called a

▲ INDIVIDUAL DUTY
According to the Bhagavad Gita, *everyone has a specific purpose, or duty, that is unique to them. Prince Arjuna was born to be a warrior, so he had to fight, regardless of how he felt and of the consequences his acts would bring.*

universal law, and we cannot make an exception under any circumstance, no matter what the consequences may be. Theories of ethics that appeal to duty are referred to as "deontological theories."

THE PROBLEM WITH INTENTIONS
The result of acting according to our duty or a universal law like always telling the truth may be positive, most of the time. However, even actions with good intentions can produce negative effects. Suppose someone found a spider stuck in a basin, and put it in a safe place where it could escape (see illustration right). We would most likely think of this as a "good" act. But what if they later found the spider dead, near to where they'd left it? We'd

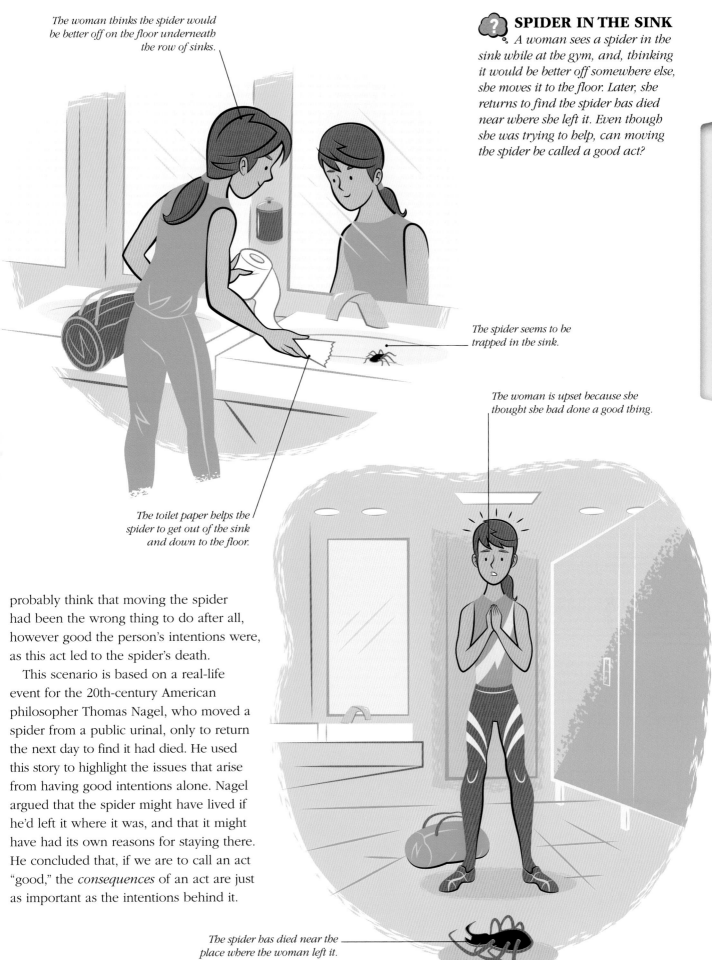

The woman thinks the spider would be better off on the floor underneath the row of sinks.

SPIDER IN THE SINK

A woman sees a spider in the sink while at the gym, and, thinking it would be better off somewhere else, she moves it to the floor. Later, she returns to find the spider has died near where she left it. Even though she was trying to help, can moving the spider be called a good act?

The spider seems to be trapped in the sink.

The woman is upset because she thought she had done a good thing.

The toilet paper helps the spider to get out of the sink and down to the floor.

probably think that moving the spider had been the wrong thing to do after all, however good the person's intentions were, as this act led to the spider's death.

This scenario is based on a real-life event for the 20th-century American philosopher Thomas Nagel, who moved a spider from a public urinal, only to return the next day to find it had died. He used this story to highlight the issues that arise from having good intentions alone. Nagel argued that the spider might have lived if he'd left it where it was, and that it might have had its own reasons for staying there. He concluded that, if we are to call an act "good," the *consequences* of an act are just as important as the intentions behind it.

The spider has died near the place where the woman left it.

129

Sudoku **Ice cream**

◀ HIGHER AND LOWER PLEASURES
What Mill called a "higher" pleasure can come from completing a math puzzle, and a "lower" pleasure is something we get from a physical activity, such as eating a treat for dessert.

THE GREATEST HAPPINESS

In the 1700s, the English philosopher Jeremy Bentham explored a theory that came to be known as utilitarianism, which states that an act is good if it brings the greatest happiness to the greatest number of people. This is called the Principle of Utility. Utilitarianism focuses *only* on the consequences of an act—weighing up the amount of pleasure and pain it will cause. The nature of the act itself or the motive of the person doing it is unimportant. It is an example of consequentialism.

Another English philosopher, John Stuart Mill, admired Bentham and, writing in the 1800s, agreed with his definition of happiness as pleasure—a hedonistic view (see pp.122–124). However, Mill analyzed not just the *quantity* of pleasure brought about by our actions, but the *quality* of it, too. He made a distinction between "higher" and "lower" pleasures. In Mill's opinion, things such as reading, writing, and learning were higher pleasures, while physical and sensory activities, such as eating and dancing, were lower pleasures. When deciding what to do, Mill encouraged us to do the things that bring about higher pleasures, instead of looking for lower ones.

THE ONE OR THE MANY

In 1967 the English philosopher Philippa Foot devised a thought experiment called The Trolley Problem to show the difference between deontology and

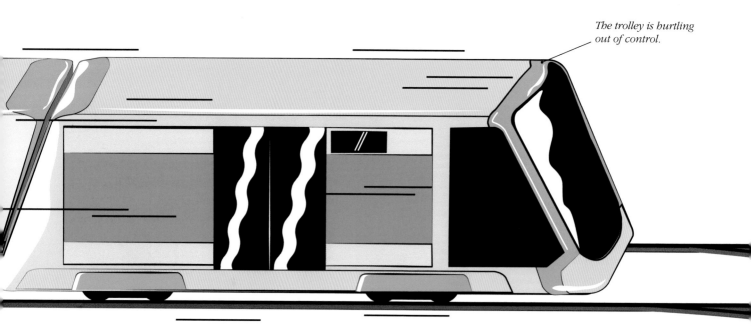

The trolley is hurtling out of control.

Could **killing** even just one person ever be thought to be **a "good" act**?

consequentialism (see illustration below). A trolley (tram) is heading down a line toward five people who are working on the tracks. They will all be killed if the trolley continues on its course. A bystander sees the situation and has access to a switch that can direct the trolley onto another line, away from the five people. However, on the other line is another worker doing some maintenance on the tracks. What is the right thing to do? A deontologist such as Kant would refer to the Categorical Imperative by asking, "What would happen if everyone thought it was alright to kill someone?" The universal law is that killing—whether it's five people or one person—is always wrong. The "good" act, therefore, might be to do nothing at all, since both options cause death. But what would we think of the person who stood by and did nothing? For consequentialists such as Bentham and Mill, the greatest happiness and the least pain is achieved by diverting the trolley onto the other line, killing one person, but saving five others. But could killing even just one person ever be thought to be a "good" act?

PART OF A WHOLE

The 20th-century Japanese philosopher Watsuji Tetsurō criticized Western ethics as being too focused on the individual, putting personal duty over relationships with

RIGHT AND WRONG

WATSUJI TETSURŌ

Philosopher Watsuji Tetsurō (1889–1960) was among a small number of Japanese thinkers to combine Eastern and Western ideas. His philosophy was initially influenced by the Western existentialist thinkers Kierkegaard, Nietzsche, and Heidegger, but then he began to consider his Japanese heritage. His views on ethics, which focus on social networks, come from his analysis of Japanese life.

others. He argued that we are all part of a huge network, with connections between each other and with the world around us. In fact, the Japanese word for ethics, *rinri*, is an amalgamation of *rin*, which means "fellows," and *ri*, which means "rational order." For Tetsurō, a good act is one that develops good relationships with fellow human beings.

THE TROLLEY PROBLEM

A trolley (tram) is heading toward five people on the tracks. A person can control a switch that could redirect the trolley to another line, where there is only one person. What should they do? Is killing one person justified in order to save the greater number of lives?

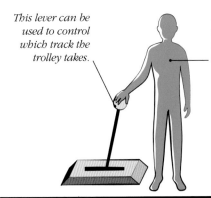

This lever can be used to control which track the trolley takes.

Should the bystander intervene and redirect the trolley to kill just one person?

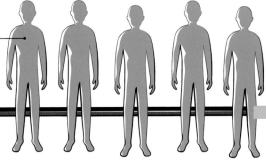

Five people will be killed if the trolley continues on this line.

This person will be killed if the trolley is diverted onto this line.

SUFFRAGETTE RALLY
Mill's work on women's rights, developed with his wife Harriet Taylor Mill, inspired the suffrage movement, which campaigned for women's right to vote. Its leader Emmeline Pankhurst, shown here in 1914, was arrested many times while protesting.

The only **freedom** which deserves the name is that of **pursuing our own good** in our own way...

John Stuart Mill

UTILITARIAN AND DEFENDER OF EQUAL RIGHTS

Through his philosophical writings and his work as a Member of Parliament, John Stuart Mill passionately defended freedom of speech, diversity, and gender equality. He was famous for promoting the values of utilitarianism, and worked toward transforming politics and society in Britain.

Born in London, England in 1806, John Stuart Mill was influenced by his father James Mill, a Scottish philosopher and historian. From a very young age, Mill studied Classics, and later history, logic, mathematics, and economic theory, all under his father—he didn't go to school or a university. The intensity of this took its toll, and at 20 Mill had what he called a "mental crisis."

THE GREATEST GOOD

Mill was interested in the philosophy of Jeremy Bentham, who was his father's friend. In Bentham's theory of utilitarianism, an action is good if it causes the greatest happiness for the greatest number of people. However, Mill later extended this philosophy, believing that people should strive for higher forms of happiness other than basic pleasure.

In 1930 Mill met Harriet Taylor and the two formed a close relationship, although they only married in 1851 after her first husband died. Taylor had a huge influence on Mill's thought, and worked with him on one of his most important works, *On Liberty* (1859), in which he argued for moral and economic freedom for everyone.

In 1865 Mill became a Member of Parliament for the Liberal Party, and in 1866 was the first person in Parliament to call for women's suffrage (the right to vote) in Britain. In his book *The Subjection of Women* (1869), he argued for gender equality—he was the first male philosopher to address this issue.

Mill died in Avignon, France in 1873. He was regarded as a major thinker in his day, whose contributions to political life paved the way for the suffragette movement in the early 1900s.

Utilitarianism states that actions are right so long as they **promote happiness.** Actions are wrong if they promote the opposite of happiness (see pp.130–131).

The **Principle of Harm** argues that an individual or government can only **restrict** someone's **freedom** in order to prevent harm to others (see p.172 and pp.194–195).

Negative liberty refers to the absence of obstacles in the way of action. **Positive liberty** is the possibility of acting to take control of your life.

To be **happy** we should pursue **higher** pleasures, such as exercising our **mind,** not just **physical** pleasures (see p.130).

Are moral values facts?

When we say "Earth is round," we know that this is a fact because we can see the evidence. However, this isn't the same for moral statements such as "people should be honest" because we have no way of proving this. If there are no facts in the world that correspond to moral values, how do we decide what is the right thing to do?

Some philosophers have identified a gap in our reasoning between "what is" (facts) and "what ought to be" (moral values), which they call the "is–ought" problem. They have analyzed this ethical issue in various ways, largely by arguing that it's difficult to derive what should be from factual or scientific evidence.

Scottish philosopher David Hume, writing in the 1700s, was skeptical about moral values. He believed that there is nothing in the way things *are* in the world that can tell us how things *ought to be*. For Hume, a factual statement such as "Elena is Spanish" can never lead to a moral one such as "Elena ought to teach Spanish." He argued that if morality is at all possible for us, it is ruled by our emotions. He insisted that morality is driven by how we feel—what he called our "passions"—rather than by reason, and that moral judgments are subjective (they are different for each person).

A red apple

Having courage

◄ **OBSERVING IN THE WORLD**
We can see the "redness" of apples, but we cannot find something in the world that matches the concept of courage. We can only observe someone being courageous.

properties, such as "red," "round," and "sweet." We can't see moral words such as "good," "bad," "right," or "wrong" in the natural world, in the same way we see the redness of an apple. If we take the redness of an apple to mean that it's a good one, i.e. "all red apples taste good," we're making an incorrect statement that Moore called "the naturalistic fallacy."

THE NATURALISTIC FALLACY

G.E. Moore, a 20th-century British philosopher, had a different approach to the "is–ought" problem. He stated that moral terms cannot be treated like natural

ETHICS AS "BOO-HOORAY"

In the 1900s, English philosopher A.J. Ayer stated that our judgments about what is good and bad are just expressions of our emotions and attitudes, an ethical theory known as emotivism. This states that when we judge something to be morally bad, it's like saying "Boo!" to show we disapprove of it, and when we think something is morally good, it's as if we're shouting "Hooray!" to show we approve of it. According to him,

We **can't see** moral words such as "right" or "wrong" in the **natural world**.

MORAL JUDGMENTS ARE JUST OPINIONS

Ayer claimed that moral statements can't be true or false. Our judgments about what is right and wrong are expressions of our emotions and attitudes.

STEALING MONEY IS WRONG!

HELPING PEOPLE IS GOOD!

By claiming that something is **morally bad**, all we are really doing is saying **"Boo!"** to indicate we **disapprove** of it.

When we judge something to be **morally good**, it's like saying **"Hooray!"** to show we **approve** of something. It's not a moral fact.

ethical statements are not factual. For example, saying "you did something wrong by stealing money" is a statement based on emotions, as opposed to simply remarking "you stole money," which can be proved by observation. Therefore, moral statements are neither true nor false, but expressions of our "boo-hooray" attitudes. A problem remains, however, in that not everybody has the same reactions—some may shout "Boo!" and others "Hooray!" to exactly the same moral situation, so this gives no basis for resolving ethical disagreements.

Do I have free will?

An important question in the study of ethics is whether we are free to do what we want—what philosophy calls having "free will." If we are *not* free to do what we want, can we be held morally responsible?

When you go to an after-school club without anyone forcing you to do so, you think you have done so freely. You could have skipped the club for a few days, for example, or decided it wasn't right for you. This is what philosophers mean by "free will." It makes you responsible for your actions, because you could have chosen to do otherwise.

IT'S ALL DECIDED FOR US

Some philosophers, such as the 17th-century Dutch philosopher Baruch Spinoza and the contemporary American thinker Sam Harris, have argued that free will does not exist—our actions are shaped by external forces. They think that things such as society, the environment, and our biology determine what we do, and we have no choice about it. This position is called "hard determinism." Hard determinists think that people can't be responsible for their actions unless those actions are the result of a free choice.

WE ARE FREE SOMETIMES

The 17th-century English philosopher Thomas Hobbes argued that determinism and free will could be compatible (exist alongside each other). He acknowledged that we are free to act according to our own will, but that we are not free to determine what that will is. This position is known as "soft determinism" or "compatibilism." This limited amount of freedom still makes us responsible for our moral choices.

WE ARE ALWAYS FREE

Existentialist philosophers (see pp.38–39) think that people have freedom of conscience (i.e. the liberty to follow their beliefs) at all times. In the 1900s, the French philosopher Jean-Paul Sartre took an extreme view when he claimed that individuals are always free,

even when they are persecuted or imprisoned, as they have the power to decide how to react to their environment. He thought free will could be a burden: we are always responsible for what we do, and this can cause great anxiety.

I CAN DO WHAT I LIKE!

I MUST FOLLOW THE RULES, AND I HAVE NO FREEDOM TO CHOOSE HOW I MOVE.

Hard determinism
This player feels that the rules of the game mean that he has **no choice** about or **responsibility** for his moves.

Free will
This player is happy to **join in** the game, and feels that the rules don't stop her making **her own choices**.

People can't be **responsible** for their actions unless those actions are **the result** of **free choice**.

THINK FOR YOURSELF

The English philosopher John Locke (see pp.56–57) said that freedom doesn't just depend on the will, but on an actual choice between alternatives. He gives the example of somebody in a locked room. Imagine it's Sunday morning and you're supposed to be going out. You feel lazy and decide to stay in bed instead. However, what you don't know is that the door of your room is locked—you couldn't have gone outside even if you'd wanted to. Can you really say that you made a "free" decision to stay in bed?

Soft determinism
This player knows she **must follow** the rules of the game, but feels that she can still **choose** what particular moves to make.

I PLAY BY THE RULES, BUT I CAN STILL MAKE SOME OF MY OWN CHOICES.

I CAN DO WHAT I LIKE, BUT THIS FREEDOM IS A BURDEN.

Existentialism
This player feels **anxious** about the moves he could make, knowing that he's **responsible** for his choices, **good and bad**.

THE FREE WILL BOARD GAME

We can think of free will as a board game played between four friends. They each represent one of the philosophical views in the debate about whether we are truly free to act, or whether our choices are determined by other factors.

THE BHAGAVAD ▶ GITA (c.400 BCE)
The ancient book of Hindu philosophy, the Gita, states that the laws of nature are in charge of all living things, and that all events are predestined.

"It is Nature that causes all movement."

"Nothing occurs at random, but everything for a reason and by necessity."

The view that all actions and events are the result of previous causes is known as determinism. Some philosophers have claimed that the sole cause is God, who decides in advance how everything should be. Others have stated that the world is governed by the inescapable laws of nature.

▲ LEUCIPPUS (c.370 BCE)
Ancient Greek philosopher Leucippus argued against the idea that things can happen randomly, and stated that everything is determined by the interactions of tiny, indivisible elements known as atoms.

DETERMINISM
versus
FREE WILL

▼ NICCOLÒ MACHIAVELLI (1469–1527)
Italian philosopher Machiavelli stated that fortune (luck) and circumstance (other conditions) are important for success, but aside from those factors, people are free to make their own choices.

Opposing the idea of determinism is the belief that humans beings have "free will." This means that everyone is able to make choices and act according to their wants and needs—there are no limitations and we are fully in control.

"God is not willing to do everything, and thus take away our free will."

"God is not the parent of evil."

◀ AUGUSTINE OF HIPPO (354–430 CE)
A Christian thinker from North Africa, St. Augustine aimed to resolve the problem of evil by claiming that people act wrongly only because they have been given free will by God.

BARUCH SPINOZA ▶
(1632–1677)
Dutch philosopher Spinoza wrote about the illusion of free will, and claimed that all things are actually decided by God.

"People are mistaken in thinking themselves free."

◀ BARON D'HOLBACH (1723–1789)
French-German philosopher d'Holbach compared the Universe to a gigantic machine, and stated that everyone within it follows its direction, having no choice of their own.

"We are all just cogs in a machine, doing what we were always meant to do."

"Free will is an illusion. Our wills are simply not of our own making."

▲ SAM HARRIS (born 1967)
American philosopher Harris argued that the intention to act arises from unknown causes. He criticized people for thinking they are important enough to have the power to choose.

JOHANN GOTTLIEB FICHTE ▶
(1762–1814)
German philosopher Fichte analyzed how people relate to one another, and he stated that an individual should keep their own "sphere of freedom" to prevent themselves from being influenced by others.

"A person can do what they ought to do; and when they say they cannot, it is because they will not."

▼ JEAN-PAUL SARTRE (1905–1980)
French existentialist Sartre insisted that an individual has no choice about being free, and is therefore ultimately responsible for their actions.

"My first act of free will shall be to believe in free will."

"A person is condemned to be free; because once they're thrown into the world, they're responsible for everything they do."

▲ WILLIAM JAMES (1842–1910)
American thinker James was a pragmatist who claimed that people's ability to choose and make decisions was proof that free will exists. He formed the idea that happiness is a choice.

Do moral values change?

Some things are considered "good" by cultures in one part of the world, but "bad" by those in another. Certain practices we now accept as morally wrong haven't always been thought of that way. If moral values change according to place or time, meaning they are relative, how do we set moral standards?

The theory that what is right and wrong is not the same for everyone, and can change over time, is called moral relativism. One of the first to think this way was the 5th-century BCE Greek philosopher Protagoras, who belonged to a group of teachers known as the sophists. He taught that morality is relative to the person making the judgment—there is no fixed moral law that applies to everyone, only social conventions (accepted ways of doing things). Therefore, it is up to individual people to decide what is ethical. Another 5th-century BCE Greek sophist, Thrasymachus, went further in observing that people with political power tend to pick and choose what is "right" according to what most benefits them, and then impose these values on others.

However, the theory of moral relativism causes certain problems. For example, how can we make someone morally or legally responsible for their actions if we can't agree on what is good and bad? Aren't some things, such as stealing, *always* wrong?

UNIVERSAL VALUES

The 4th-century BCE Greek philosopher Plato and the 17th-century thinker Immanuel Kant thought so. They argued that morality must be universal—the goodness of an action has to be the same across all of humanity and across all generations. This means that when, for example, we say "slavery is wrong" we state it as a fact. Moral values are not a matter of people's opinions or what is in their interest. They are objective.

> ## Humankind is the **measure** of **all things**.
> **PROTAGORAS**, c.490–c.420 BCE

YUM!

I DON'T LIKE CHEESE

Unlike the woman, the man **loves cheese**, so Cheese Galore is **his winner**. The well-balanced Perfect Portion doesn't appeal to the boy who **only eats pasta**.

WHERE'S THE PASTA?

CHEESE GALORE

PERFECT PORTION

WHO DECIDES OUR VALUES?

If moral values are universal, there is still the question of where they come from. Many philosophers throughout history have argued that the source of morality is God. Their argument is that because God is by nature good, goodness in an action has to come from God's will (see p.152). More recently, philosophers have come up with two more theories of moral relativism. Thinkers who believe in moral evolutionism say that what we call "good" and "bad" has evolved with the human species over thousands of years, independently of our belief in God. The contemporary American philosopher T.M. Scanlon has developed a theory called contractualism. He argues that what we accept to be right and wrong is the result of a type of "contract" between people in a society, in which we all have an unspoken agreement on how we behave toward one another.

You're on vacation when you become very ill. At the hospital, there is a long line of people waiting to see the doctor. However, someone tells you that it is the custom here to offer money—a bribe—in order to be seen right away. Waiting your turn could put your health at risk, but offering the bribe might mean that someone else doesn't get the treatment they need. Is there an objectively "right" thing to do in these circumstances?

DELICIOUS MEAL CONTEST

One of these judges **likes** to eat **insects**, which are not to everyone's taste. The other doesn't **eat meat**, so she won't even try the Meat Medley.

The **head judge** has to **reach a decision** with the help of the other judges, but how can she do so when they all have **different** opinions?

HOW CAN WE AGREE?

THAT LOOKS TASTY!

I'M A VEGETARIAN!

IT'S ALL RELATIVE
The six judges for the delicious meal contest are having trouble deciding which is the winning dish. There is no universal agreement on which is the "best" meal, because what is delicious is relative to their personal taste.

INSECT SURPRISE

MEAT MEDLEY

Why is ethics relevant?

Philosophers throughout history have tried to guide us on how to behave morally. In our ever-changing world, there are always issues that are in need of ethical analysis, such as animal rights, climate change, and world poverty. Understanding why these issues are relevant helps us decide how to respond to them.

Some of the world's problems may be things that affect us directly, such as pollution and climate change. These problems may have responses that are relatively easy to achieve, such as trying to recycle more. Other problems may involve people and places that seem very far from our own lives, and we may wonder whether there is anything we can do about them.

ANIMAL RIGHTS

The issue of animal rights affects us today, but people were also concerned about this thousands of years ago. The ancient Indian philosophy of *ahimsā*, which means "noninjury" (i.e. not to harm others), is central to Hinduism and Buddhism. It promotes the virtue of compassion, calling all human beings to avoid violence, including toward animals. Many people claim that a commitment to *ahimsā* implies we should be vegetarian, and shouldn't kill animals for food.

Contemporary Australian philosopher Peter Singer is a vegetarian who is best-known for championing animal rights. He argues that animals have a right to their existence, and to be protected from the harm caused by humans—animals shouldn't be used as things we can buy and dispose of whenever we feel like it. As a utilitarian, Singer believes that actions should always bring about the least amount of suffering—and therefore the greatest happiness—to the greatest number (see p.130). In Singer's view, this philosophy should also apply to animals, not just to human beings.

ENVIRONMENTAL ACTIVISM

The 20th-century Norwegian philosopher Arne Naess was also an environmental campaigner who criticized the huge negative impact of human interference in the natural world. He noted that nature depends on a complex network of relationships. Thinking that humans are central to this network leads people to behave unethically. In 1973 Naess wrote about "deep ecology," ecological and environmental ethics based on the claim that both human and nonhuman life on Earth has intrinsic and equal value, and that humankind should stop regarding nature as simply useful to us.

▲ POLLUTED ENVIRONMENT
Naess was concerned with the excessive use of natural resources and pollution. To avoid environmental catastrophe, he asked us to recognize that we are only a part of nature, and not to behave as if we were at the center of it.

We are **responsible** not only for what **we do** but also for what **we could have prevented**.

PETER SINGER, *Writings on an Ethical Life* (2000)

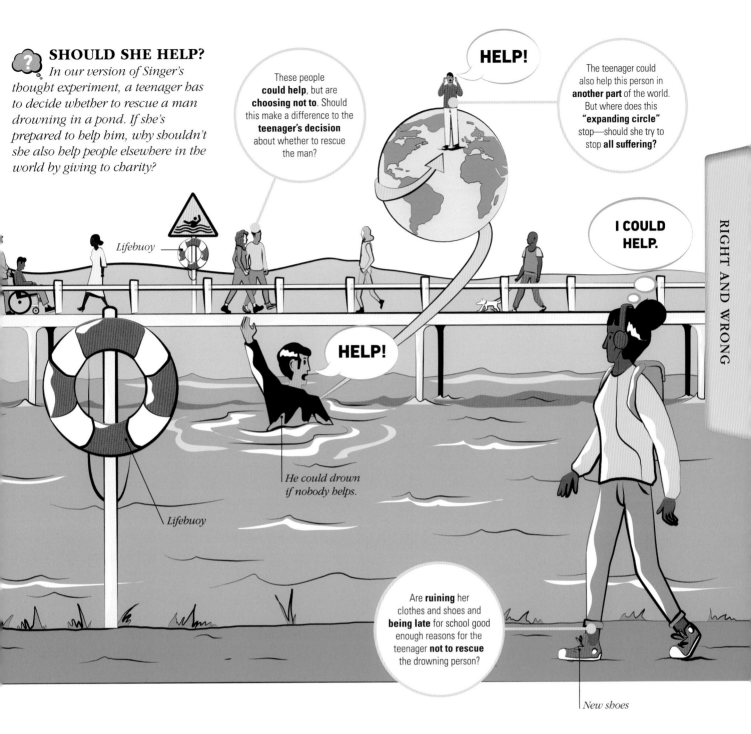

BEING CHARITABLE

In addition to animal rights, Peter Singer has turned his attention to world poverty. He believes that people who have enough money have a moral duty to use their wealth to reduce poverty simply because they can. For instance, think of all the things you own—games, clothes, books. How many of those do you think you could use to help people without significantly reducing your own well-being? However, Singer acknowledges that people are often willing to help those people or causes that are close to them, but find it more difficult to do so for those that are more distant.

Singer devised a thought experiment called The Drowning Child and the Expanding Circle (1997) to help make his point. Imagine a teenager sees a man drowning in a pond on her way to school (see illustration above). She knows she could easily save him, but her clothes and new shoes will get muddy in the process, and she'll be late for school. What should she do? Most people would think that a human life is worth more than ruined clothes and shoes. They would probably think that we have a duty to rescue someone if we can, as long as we don't put ourselves in danger. Singer then states that if we have a duty to someone right in front of us, we also have one to those in our wider community, as well as to those who are suffering far away—even more so when we have resources to spare. He refers to this as the "expanding circle" of charity.

RELIGION

The philosophy of religion examines important religious matters through reasoning rather than faith. Western philosophers have argued the case for and against the existence of God, and discussed what attributes this God might have. Throughout the world, a central debate in the philosophy of religion is the question of why evil exists. Many thinkers have also discussed the relationship between reasoning and faith.

Does God exist?

Many religions around the world have at their core a belief in one or more divine beings, who are often seen as benevolent creators of the Universe. In Western philosophy of religion, which tends to focus on the God of Judaism, of Christianity, and of Islam, many thinkers have used reasoning to try to prove or disprove the existence of such a being.

Benevolent Well-meaning, helpful, and kindly.

Morality Principles that determine right from wrong, as well as what is considered good and bad behavior.

Virtue An excellent quality in a person, such as courage or honesty.

There have been many proofs given for God's existence over the centuries. Many rely on arguments that God is necessary in some way. For instance, some proofs argue that God is the creator or cause of the Universe, while others say that concepts such as perfection and morality would mean nothing without the existence of God.

GOD AS FIRST CAUSE

In the 4th century BCE, the ancient Greek philosopher Aristotle argued that everything that is in motion must have been moved by something else. Object A was moved by object B, which in turn was moved by object C. But this series of "moved movers" cannot go back infinitely. At some point, said Aristotle, there must be an "unmoved mover" responsible for all the movement that followed in the Universe. According to Aristotle, this unmoved mover, and the Universe itself, must be eternal.

▲ FALLING DOMINOES
In the sequence of dominoes shown above, the finger pushing on the first domino causes all the other dominoes to fall. The cosmological argument says that God is this "first cause" for everything that happens in the Universe.

Early Christian thinkers tried to combine Aristotle's ideas with their beliefs. But they disagreed that the Universe was eternal, and argued that it had a beginning. In the 9th century, the Muslim thinker Al-Kindi took this further and argued that everything that has a beginning has a cause. Therefore the Universe must have a cause—and that cause is God. This is known as the cosmological argument for the existence of God. The 13th-century Italian philosopher and Catholic priest Thomas Aquinas argued that the first cause that started everything, or God, did not itself need to have a cause, because God exists outside the Universe, and is eternal.

While the cosmological argument attempts to prove the existence of an extremely powerful God, it says nothing about whether this God is an all-knowing or supremely benevolent being.

REASONING GOD INTO EXISTENCE

The 11th-century Christian archbishop and philosopher Anselm of Canterbury came up with a very different argument for God's existence. His proof is a version of what is known as the ontological argument. This is an argument for God's existence that relies solely on reason—rather than on observations about the Universe. Anselm started his argument by defining God as the greatest being it is possible to imagine. Anselm argued that something that exists in reality is greater than something that exists only in the imagination. So a God that exists in reality must be greater than one that only exists as an idea. This means that God must exist, because otherwise we can imagine something greater than the greatest thing we can imagine, which doesn't make sense.

Many later thinkers have found the ontological argument to be unsatisfactory. The French monk Gaunilo, a contemporary of Anselm, was one of the first to criticize it. He said that using the same reasoning you

I DON'T BELIEVE that God exists.

But do you agree that if God did exist, that being would be the **GREATEST POSSIBLE BEING** that could be **IMAGINED**?

Yes, I suppose that's **TRUE**.

And is it **POSSIBLE TO IMAGINE** such a being as God?

It's possible to **IMAGINE** such a being, certainly. But that doesn't mean God **EXISTS**.

And **WHAT IS GREATER**: something that exists only in the **IMAGINATION**, or something that also exists in **REALITY**?

Something that **EXISTS IN REALITY**. An ice cream in my hand is better than one in my mind.

So if God **ONLY EXISTS IN THE IMAGINATION**, then we can imagine a being that is **GREATER THAN THE GREATEST BEING** we can imagine.

But that **DOESN'T MAKE ANY SENSE**!

Exactly! So **GOD MUST EXIST**.

ANSELM AND THE FOOL

Anselm believed that even a fool would have to agree that they could imagine a godlike being, even if they didn't believe that God actually exists. This is the starting point for Anselm's ontological argument.

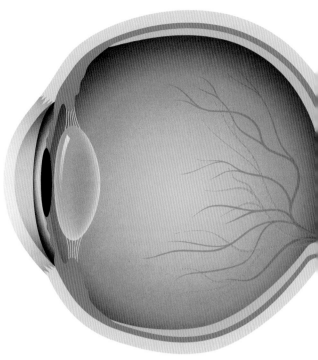

▲ THE DIVINE WATCHMAKER

In the same way that the intricate workings inside a watch imply its design by a watchmaker, Paley argued, the complex structure of objects in nature (such as the human eye) implies some form of divine designer.

could, for example, attempt to prove the existence of a perfect island, greater than any island that could be imagined. But while you can have an idea of this perfect island, that doesn't mean that it exists.

THE DESIGN ARGUMENT

Some arguments for the existence of God have looked at the world around us for evidence of a designer. In the 1700s, the English priest William Paley developed a famous version of the design argument. He compared aspects of the natural world to a watch—a device that was as high-tech in Paley's day as a modern smartphone is to us. Paley said if you found a watch, you'd know that someone had designed it. He argued that many things that exist in nature are just as complex, or even more complex, than a watch, and so must have been created by design. How else, for example, could the human eye be so well-suited to seeing? Paley concluded that it must have been designed by God.

There have been many powerful objections to this argument. The 18th-century Scottish philosopher David Hume said that even if the human eye had a designer, that designer wasn't necessarily God. It could have been designed by a lesser being, or one that no longer exists. At best the design argument, if it is accepted, proves that an extremely intelligent designer existed when the eye was designed.

One of the most powerful objections to the design argument came from the world of science. Paley wrote his argument more than 50 years before Charles Darwin first presented his theory of evolution. Darwin's theory gives an explanation of how nature becomes more complex over time, slowly evolving on its own, without a designer. However, many religious people believe that God is responsible for evolution.

THE MORAL ARGUMENT

The 18th-century German philosopher Immanuel Kant placed morality at the center of his argument for God's existence. Kant believed that the goal of human existence is to find happiness through virtue. He argued that an afterlife must exist so that those who live virtuously can be rewarded with happiness, and this afterlife must have been created by God.

◀ MORAL COMPASS

One version of the moral argument says that moral values such as goodness would not be meaningful if God didn't exist. It would be impossible for us to say what is good without God, just as it's impossible to find North without a compass.

The Northern Irish writer C.S. Lewis gave a simpler version of the moral argument. He said that we all have a conscience that helps us to know what is right and wrong—and the best explanation for the existence of this conscience is that it was put in us by a moral lawgiver, or God. Nonbelievers disagree, and say that morality is a human invention.

ARGUING AGAINST GOD

There have been many attempts to prove the existence of God through reasoning, but philosophers have also argued against God's existence. The 19th-century German philosopher Ludwig Feuerbach rejected the Christian belief that humans were created in God's image, and instead suggested that humans create God in their own image. They do this by projecting ideal human qualities onto an imaginary being. Feuerbach argued that we should stop doing this, and instead focus on being better people ourselves.

The 20th-century English philosopher Bertrand Russell said that people who don't believe in God are not required to prove that God doesn't exist. The burden of proof lies with those who believe. Russell asked us to imagine that a person believes that there is a china teapot orbiting the Sun, somewhere between the Earth and Mars. The teapot is so small that no telescopes are powerful enough to help us see it. The person could not really expect anybody else to share their belief without proof. It would be more appropriate to assume the teapot doesn't exist. Russell believes the same applies to belief in the existence of God—without any proof, it is better to assume that God doesn't exist.

GAMBLING ON GOD

Is there any advantage to believing in God? According to the 17th-century French philosopher Blaise Pascal, yes there is. He developed what is known as "Pascal's Wager," an argument that favors belief. Pascal said that you should gamble on God existing. If you are right and God does exist, your reward is eternal happiness. And if you are wrong and God doesn't exist, you won't lose anything. But if you gamble on God not existing, and you're right, you won't gain anything—but if you're wrong, you risk an eternity of punishment.

The American philosopher William James joked that if he were God, he'd prevent those who believed in him because of Pascal's Wager from entering Heaven. Gambling on God's existence seems to be the wrong sort of reason for religious belief.

RUSSELL'S TEAPOT

According to Russell, there is no way of disproving that a teapot orbits the Sun between the Earth and Mars, just as there is no way to disprove the existence of God. But just because the existence of either of these things can't be disproved, it doesn't mean that there is any reason to believe that they do exist.

NONREALISM

Some philosophers, including the contemporary English thinker Don Cupitt, have argued that when people say "I believe in God," they aren't claiming that a being exists in the same sense that a real person exists. Rather they are committing themselves to a way of living, an optimistic outlook, and a set of rituals and myths that embody that faith. Critics of this non-ealist approach argue this is just a form of atheism—the lack of belief in God—by another name.

A child enters the faith of the Coptic Orthodox Church during a ritual of baptism in Egypt

Everything owes its existence to **God**, including **Christian belief** and **philosophy**. The two can therefore always work together **without contradiction**.

Something can be **created by God** and at the same time it can have **existed forever** (see p.146).

The **soul continues to exist** after the **death** and **decay** of the **body**.

Nothing can be known, save what is true.

Thomas Aquinas

BROUGHT TOGETHER PHILOSOPHY AND CHRISTIAN THOUGHT

Italian philosopher Thomas Aquinas was also a Catholic priest. He followed a school of philosophy developed by Christian thinkers known as Scholasticism. His teachings demonstrated that philosophy could be combined with Christian doctrine, as both human reason and religious beliefs came from God.

Aquinas was born in c.1225 in the castle of Roccasecca, Italy. He spent his childhood in a monastery, training to become a Benedictine monk—a person who took religious vows based on the teachings of Benedict of Nursia. He was sent to Naples at the age of 13, where he studied the works of the ancient Greek thinker Aristotle (see pp.22–23), which influenced him. Six years later, Aquinas joined the Dominican order of monks. This was against the wishes of his family, who wanted him to remain in the Benedictine order, so they kidnapped and imprisoned him in the family castle for almost a year. However, he defied them by returning to the Dominican order following his release in 1245.

ARISTOTLE'S INFLUENCE

Aquinas became a priest in 1250 and taught theology (the study of relgious belief) at the University of Paris. In contrast to many in the Church at that time, Aquinas believed that Aristotle's philosophy did not contradict Christian teaching, but helped explain it. For example, Aristotle claimed that the Universe had no beginning.

ILLUMINATED MANUSCRIPT ▶
Monks used to write out and decorate books by hand, such as this page from Summa Theologiae. *These are known as "illuminated manuscripts".*

Aquinas argued that this was the case, and that God had created the Universe in such a way that it had always existed. Aquinas wrote many books, and in his most famous (unfinished) work, *Summa Theologiae* (1265), he refers to Aristotle as "The Philosopher," showing how much he was inspired by Aristotle's work.

A year before his death, Aquinas confessed that he had experienced a heavenly vision that revealed all secrets to him, and he never wrote again. He died in 1274, and was recognized as a saint by Pope John XXII in 1323. Aquinas never thought of himself as a philosopher. But his writings helped to keep philosophy at the heart of medieval Christian thought.

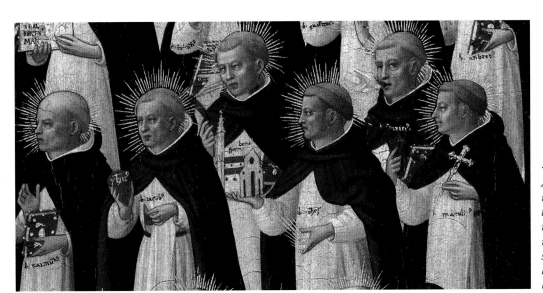

◀ DOMINICAN FRIARS
At the age of 19, Aquinas ran away from home to join the Dominican Order, which was founded by St. Dominic in 1216. The order's priests, shown here, are sometimes known as the "Black Friars" because of their black cloaks.

What is the nature of God?

The religions of Judaism, Christianity, and Islam all believe in the existence of the same single god, and hold that this god is the creator of the Universe. But what is God like? This question goes beyond describing the form that God takes, if God can even be said to have a form. It is also asking about God's role in the Universe. Philosophers of religion in different traditions have debated the nature of God for hundreds of years.

How involved is God in the Universe? Most followers of monotheistic religions such as Judaism, Christianity, and Islam are theists. They believe that God not only created the Universe, but also oversees it, intervening in events and human lives. But some believers are deists, who hold that God is the creator of everything, but does not intervene.

GOD IS PERFECT

Medieval theist philosophers of religion made certain assumptions about God. They believed that God is a perfect being, all-good, all-knowing, and all-powerful (see box below). Many thinkers have found problems with these attributes and how they interact. For example, if God is good, and knows everything that will happen, why doesn't God prevent people from doing evil? This is known as the problem of evil (see p.155). The 13th-century Italian philosopher Thomas Aquinas responded by saying that God exists far beyond human understanding. Nothing we say about God is literally true—it's just our best approximation.

GOD IS EVERYTHING

The 17th-century Jewish Dutch philosopher Baruch Spinoza did not see God as a separate entity with its own attributes. His ideas about God are a form of

ATTRIBUTES OF GOD

Medieval philosophers of religion such as Augustine of Hippo and Thomas Aquinas believed that God is perfect. They identified a number of attributes that make up this perfection. These attributes became generally accepted in Christianity, Judaism, and Islam.

Omnipotent	God is all-powerful.
Omniscient	God knows everything.
Omnibenevolent	God has infinite goodness.
Omnipresent	God is everywhere at once.
Omnitemporal	God exists in all times at once.

◀ WHAT GOD IS NOT
Many philosophers have argued that God is beyond human understanding. Maimonides claimed that there is nothing meaningful we can say about what God is—we can only talk about what God is not.

MOSES MAIMONIDES

Originally named Moses Ben Maimon, Moses Maimonides (1138–1204) was a Jewish philosopher. Born in Córdoba in modern-day Spain, he began writing at the age of 23 on the subjects of religion, philosophy, and medicine. His writings helped to introduce the theories of Aristotle into medieval religious philosophy. Maimonides is regarded as one of the greatest Jewish philosophers. His ideas had a huge influence on medieval Christian thought.

pantheism, which views God and everything in the Universe as one and the same. Spinoza was expelled from his synagogue (a Jewish place of worship) for his ideas, which were seen as a kind of atheism. According to his colleagues, saying that God is in everything, and therefore impersonal, is almost the same as saying that God doesn't exist. In the 1900s, the physicist Albert Einstein said that he believed in Spinoza's idea of God, not in a God who cares about human beings.

GOD IS UNKNOWABLE

Other philosophers have argued that there is no way for us to know what God is like. The 9th-century Muslim Arab philosopher Al-Kindi believed that God is "pure unity," a oneness, something that can't be described and explained through its parts. We can know that God exists as the cause of everything, but no more than this.

Moses Maimonides, a 12th-century Jewish thinker, believed that God's attributes couldn't be listed. In *A Guide for the Perplexed* (1190), he claimed that people can only say what God is not. For example, God is "non-corporeal" (has no body) and isn't found in any particular place. He said that passages in the Torah (the first five books of the Hebrew Bible) which seem to describe God's hands, or God being in a garden, aren't literal accounts, but stories to help us understand God.

The 15th-century Christian thinker Nicholas of Cusa took the view that God is too difficult for humans to understand. Believers should have faith in God's existence but try not to define God. Critics of Nicholas's view argue that if people can't understand what God is like, how are they to know whether or not God exists?

GOD IS NATURE
According to Spinoza there is only one substance in the Universe and that substance is God. This means that God must be in everything: the sky, mountains, plants, and all that exists in nature.

Why does evil exist?

Sometimes the world can appear to be full of tragedies and disasters—events or actions that many people call "evil." The nature of good and evil is a central topic in many religions around the world, so the question of why evil exists has been an important one for philosophers of religion throughout history.

According to some philosophers, there is a difference between natural evil, such as earthquakes, storms, and disease, and the moral evil that humans do to each other through war, torture, and other kinds of cruelty. Moral evil can sometimes make natural evil worse, for example when a government fails to help their people in a natural disaster, such as during a famine. While some philosophers have attempted to explain the existence of natural evil, many more have concerned themselves with the nature of moral evil.

A WORLD OF SUFFERING

Some Eastern philosophies see evil as a natural part of the world. Buddhism, a religion originating in ancient India, recognizes no all-powerful god. It has at its heart the belief that there is great suffering in the world. To be aware that suffering exists is the first of Four Noble Truths, a series of teachings that lead the believer out of suffering.

The ancient Chinese Daoist philosopher Laozi also regarded suffering as a natural part of life. He argued that the world is completely indifferent to us, and we interpret things as evil because of our human point of view. Laozi said that nature does not treat people with either cruelty or kindness, but like "straw dogs"—objects of no importance.

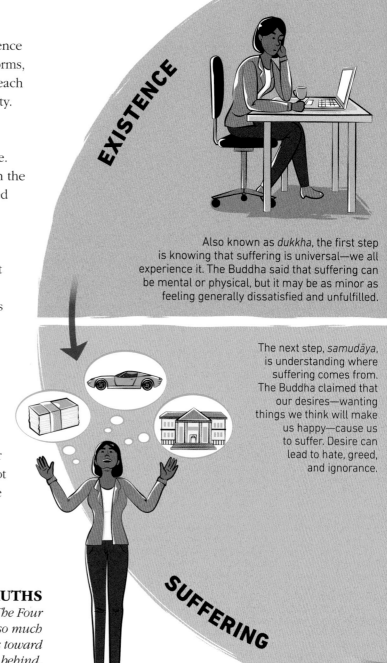

EXISTENCE

Also known as *dukkha*, the first step is knowing that suffering is universal—we all experience it. The Buddha said that suffering can be mental or physical, but it may be as minor as feeling generally dissatisfied and unfulfilled.

The next step, *samudāya*, is understanding where suffering comes from. The Buddha claimed that our desires—wanting things we think will make us happy—cause us to suffer. Desire can lead to hate, greed, and ignorance.

SUFFERING

THE FOUR NOBLE TRUTHS
Central to the teachings of Buddhism are The Four Noble Truths. They explain why there is so much suffering in the world, and guide believers toward a path that leaves suffering behind.

JARGON BUSTER

Moral Concerned with standards of right and wrong, and good and bad behavior.

Free will The power to act by choice without being restricted by fate or by a superior force.

Omnipotent Having great and unlimited power.

THE PROBLEM OF EVIL

For those religions with a god who takes an interest in our welfare, such as Christianity or Judaism, the existence of evil is harder to explain. An all-knowing and all-good God must be aware of evil and would want to prevent it, and an all-powerful God could stop it. So why is there evil? In philosophy, this question is known as the Problem of Evil.

Some thinkers respond to the Problem of Evil by arguing that perhaps God is not all-knowing, all-good, and all-powerful. In the religion of Manicheism, for example, evil is explained by an ongoing struggle between God and the Devil. In this view God is powerful, but not

HANNAH ARENDT

German-American Hannah Arendt (1906–1975) was a Jewish thinker who fled Germany in 1933 to avoid persecution. In 1961 she attended the trial of the Nazi Adolf Eichmann who had planned the train schedules that sent millions of Jews to their deaths. At the trial Arendt said he didn't seem to be a monster, but was "terrifyingly normal," despite the horrific crimes he was accused of. She called this "the banality of evil."

omnipotent. Many atheists go one step further, and say that the existence of evil in the world proves that God doesn't exist.

EVIL AND FREE WILL

Some religious thinkers believe that evil exists because God has given people free will—the ability to choose. The 2nd-century Christian bishop Irenaeus claimed that free will is necessary. God created a world that includes evil because it allows us to choose goodness and become better people.

The medieval Christian philosopher Augustine of Hippo also believed in a God-given free will, and claimed that evil is simply the absence of goodness. God doesn't create evil, and so isn't responsible for it. People create evil by acting wrongly, using their free will to behave immorally and against God's guidance.

FREE TO CHOOSE ▶
Many philosophers have argued that we are not under the control of some divine being, like puppets on strings. God gave us free will to choose our own actions, whether for good or for evil.

EIGHTFOLD PATH

The final step, *magga*, is the Buddha's list of instructions to end suffering. He devised the Eightfold Path, which includes right action, thought, and speech, to guide people toward spiritual enlightenment—*nirvana*.

Taking action to end suffering is the step known as *nirodha*. Desire is seen as a destructive fire that should be extinguished. To do this, the Buddha advised believers to liberate themselves from their worldly attachments, such as the objects they love.

ATTACHMENT

155

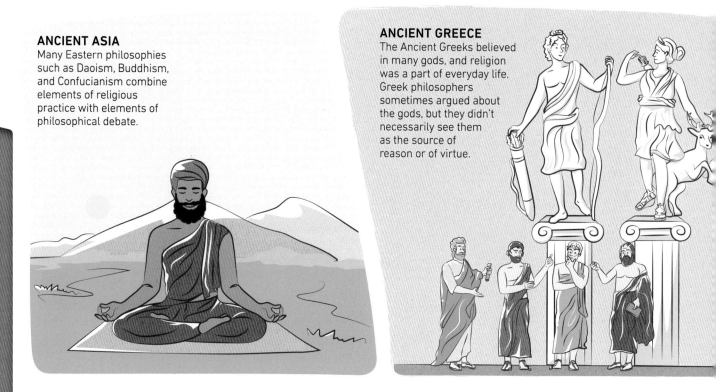

ANCIENT ASIA
Many Eastern philosophies such as Daoism, Buddhism, and Confucianism combine elements of religious practice with elements of philosophical debate.

ANCIENT GREECE
The Ancient Greeks believed in many gods, and religion was a part of everyday life. Greek philosophers sometimes argued about the gods, but they didn't necessarily see them as the source of reason or of virtue.

Can reason and faith be united?

Religious faith usually involves belief in a higher power or powers, and this faith influences the believer's way of life. But in the philosophy of religion, all beliefs are examined using reasoning. Whether or not faith can survive when challenged by reason has been a source of much philosophical debate.

Some thinkers claim that faith and reason are not opposed if they are used together to explore truth. Some philosophers favor faith over reason, saying that this faith leads to understanding, while others argue that reason comes before faith. Other thinkers argue that belief in a god or gods must be in conflict with rational thinking because this belief leads to contradictions.

FAITH BEFORE REASON

In his book *Proslogion* (1077–1078), Italian-born thinker Anselm of Canterbury wrote *credo ut intelligam*—Latin for "I believe so that I might understand." Anselm suggested that faith provides a "path" to understanding, and that it is not possible to know God without first having belief.

In the 1800s the Danish philosopher Søren Kierkegaard also put faith before reason. Kierkegaard saw faith as an intense personal commitment to religion. He believed that while faith is a more difficult path to follow than reason, it is a path that it is more important to pursue. Kierkegaard saw faith as superior to reason, partly because it involves a leap into the unknown and demands a special kind of trust in God.

REASON BEFORE FAITH

The medieval Arab Muslim thinker Ibn Rushd argued that careful reasoning leads to truth. It is an illusion to say that reason and faith are in conflict—they are simply two different ways of arriving at the same truth.

CHRISTIAN EUROPE
Between the 5th and 15th centuries, the Catholic Church held authority over people's beliefs and way of life across Europe. Religion was seen as superior to philosophy.

THE GOLDEN AGE OF ISLAM
From the 9th to the 12th centuries, Islamic scholars studied ancient Greek philosophy, and made great advances in science and mathematics. They didn't see their faith as incompatible with rational thought.

TOGETHER AND APART
Throughout human history religious beliefs and rational thinking have existed alongside one another. They have either been considered as separate and contradictory, or complementary ways of reaching meaningful truths.

THE SECULAR WORLD
From the 1500s, a scientific revolution took place across Europe. It challenged many religious beliefs, and the Catholic Church lost much of its power over society. The idea grew that rational thought and religious faith were entirely separate.

However, Ibn Rushd claimed that some claims in religious texts are to be interpreted as poetic, rather than literal, truths.

Like Ibn Rushd, the medieval Irish Catholic thinker Johannes Scotus Eriugena argued for the importance of reason. But Eriugena believed that philosophical reasoning isn't a separate tool that is used to understand religion. Instead, religion and philosophy are one and the same thing. For Eriugena, reason is not in conflict with faith, but supports it.

REASON WITHOUT FAITH
In recent years some atheists (people who believe no god exists), including the zoologist Richard Dawkins, have argued faith to be a kind of delusion (a mistaken belief), and that reason should be separated from faith altogether. According to Dawkins, reason and science support atheism, not religion. Most atheists believe that there is powerful evidence against the existence of the divine, and that science provides far more reliable truths than committing to a religious way of life.

> # The **true philosophy** is the true religion, and the **true religion** is the true philosophy.
> **JOHANNES SCOTUS ERIUGENA**, *Treatise on Divine Predestination* (800s)

SOCIETY

The study of how we live together in societies and how those in power behave is known as political philosophy. From the earliest times, thinkers have discussed ways to improve society, and their theories have had a huge impact on political systems across the world. The issues at the heart of these theories, such as freedom and equality, are still being fought for today.

Why do societies form?

Societies are groups of people who live together, organizing themselves according to shared rules and values. Philosophers have explored the different ways we form societies, and the different types of political system that can result.

Plato was the first ancient Greek political philosopher. In his famous work the *Republic* (c.375 BCE), Plato suggested that all human beings have special talents that make them suited to join one of three groups: producers, auxiliaries, and guardians. The producers have the ability to create; they include craftspeople and farmers. The auxiliaries are people who make good soldiers. The guardians are

PERICLES ▶
A gifted political leader like the ancient Greek general Pericles, who ruled Athens just prior to Plato's birth, would have made a great "guardian" in Plato's ideal society.

best at ruling. Plato thought people should form a city (*polis*) to work together, creating an ideal society that would make the best use of people's talents.

OUR NATURAL STATE

Later philosophers proposed that before there were human societies, people lived in a "state of nature." What this real or imagined state might have been like depended on their view of human nature.

Xunzi, a 3rd-century BCE Chinese Confucian thinker, believed that people are naturally amoral (without a sense of right and wrong) and, without education and social rules to follow, collapse into disagreement and disorder. The 17th-century English philosopher Thomas Hobbes held a similar view and, in a now famous phrase, described life in the state of nature as "solitary, poor, nasty, brutish, and short."

Chinese Confucian thinker Mencius, writing in the 4th century BCE, had a more positive view of people.

He believed that humankind is naturally good, but that the role of society was to nurture this goodness. The 17th-century English philosopher John Locke also thought that people are good, and that they are rational. He suggested that people in a state of nature could live happily and enjoy things such as property ownership, but might still have disputes. Jean-Jacques Rousseau, an 18th-century French philosopher, had a high opinion of people, thinking they are equal to one another, free, and not inclined to disagree. However, he thought people became corrupted by the growth of inequality—the result of some owning more property than others.

AGREEING TO BE RULED

Hobbes, Locke, and Rousseau used their descriptions of human nature as a starting point to determine why societies form and what benefits people would get from living in one. These philosophers thought that forming a society is like making a "social contract" between the

THOMAS HOBBES

English philosopher Thomas Hobbes (1588–1679) was heavily influenced by his experience of the English Civil War (1642–1651), which was fought between supporters of parliament and supporters of the king. Hobbes was on the side of the monarchy, which made him unpopular with the parliamentarians, who seemed certain to win the war, and so in 1640 Hobbes fled to Paris. He later fell out of favor there, returning to England in 1651. Hobbes used his most famous work, *Leviathan*, to justify royal power as a system of government for all.

	Hobbes	Locke	Rousseau
What human nature is like	Selfish, violent, and evil	Rational and good	Good and compassionate, but can be corrupted
What the state of nature is like	Brutal, with disorder and war	Peaceful, with occasional disagreement	Equal, free, and peaceful, but inequalites could arise
What kind of ruler is needed	All-powerful ruler who cannot be overthrown	Ruler or elected government that can be overthrown	The people themselves, voting directly on how society is run

people and their ruler—an agreement as to what benefits people can expect, and what they need to do in return. They each described how societies can maintain order and help resolve disputes, but they had different ideas on what system of rule would be needed to achieve this (see pp.164–167).

Forming a society is like making a "social contract"…

THE SOCIAL CONTRACT

The idea of a "social contract" is that people are originally free from society and live in a "state of nature," but they agree to be ruled so that they can benefit from all the things that society brings.

Jean-Jacques Rousseau

CHAMPION OF FREEDOM

The son of a watchmaker, Jean-Jacques Rousseau was a Genevan philosopher who rose to fame from modest beginnings. He became well known in France, where he was celebrated for his political writings, but was later persecuted.

Jean-Jacques Rousseau was born in 1712 in Geneva (now in Switzerland). His mother died days after his birth, leaving Rousseau to be brought up by his father. When he was five, his father sold their expensive family house and they moved into a smaller apartment to live among craftsmen. Geneva was a republic where all male citizens could, in theory, vote on every policy. In practice, power belonged only to a small number of wealthy families. Rousseau grew up witnessing his poor neighbors protesting for change.

Abandoned by his father at the age of 10, Rousseau made his own way into high society through friends and acquaintances. At one time he worked for French Baroness Françoise-Louise de Warens, who introduced him to philosophy, math, and music.

RISE AND FALL

Rousseau went to Paris in 1742, and was first known as a composer. While he was there, he became part of the movement known as the Enlightenment, which involved a group of leading thinkers exchanging ideas on philosophy and science. In 1750 Rousseau won a competition with his essay *Discourse on the Sciences and the Arts*. This brought him significant fame, and his major books on political philosophy followed: *Discourse on Inequality* (1755), *The Social Contract*, and *Émile* (both in 1762). These examined the natural instincts of human beings and advised on how best to construct a fairer society, but his writings angered the Parisian authorities who ordered his arrest.

Rousseau fled to England but soon returned to France in secret. During this time he worked on his autobiography, *Confessions*. Rousseau died a wanted man in 1778 while hiding in the estates of the great French nobleman, the Marquis de Girardin. However, his ideas were to become influential in the French Revolution (1789–1799), and in the Romantic movement of the 18th and 19th centuries.

People are **born good**. Poorly formed **governments corrupt them**, and this leads to tension and **disorder** (see pp.160–161).

Feelings are part of our **natural instincts** that should be used as a **guide** to life, instead of reason.

Society bases its **laws** on what it believes is the **general will"** of the people, but this is not the actual desire of any individual.

Education should not aim to **discipline** or repress children's natural tendencies, but to **encourage** their expression and development.

FRENCH REVOLUTION
Rousseau's ideas had a big impact on 18th-century politics, and his views on who should rule and how laws should be made inspired the leaders of the French Revolution. Here, rioters attack the Royal Palace during one of several uprisings.

Humankind is **born free**, and everywhere **is in chains.**

Who should have power?

When people live in a society, they need to think about what kind of rule to agree to, and how much power that person or state should have. Philosophers have analyzed these issues, and have also discussed how people can ensure that the ruling power fulfils its duties—and determine what can be done if it doesn't. Ideas about power and who should have it are constantly evolving.

In the 4th century BCE, the ancient Greek philosopher Plato thought that political power should be given exclusively to those most expert in ruling, a group of people he called "guardians" (see p.160). For him, philosophers would make ideal guardians, as they were best at answering questions such as "What is justice?." Plato thought that those who weren't very interested in having power were the best ones to be given it. Being interested only in ideas, it was unlikely that these "philosophers-kings" would be corrupted by, say, a desire for money. He imagined this scenario as an ideal government that would last forever, so he didn't really build any safeguards into it. There was no possibility for people to change the system in case things went wrong, for example, which now seems somewhat authoritarian.

Hobbes named his all-powerful ruler "Leviathan" after a giant sea serpent that appears in the Bible.

The sword symbolizes the power of the monarch.

ABSOLUTE POWER

The English philosopher Thomas Hobbes, in his famous book *Leviathan* (1651), wrote that the most important goal of the state was maintaining order among the people. Everything else was less important than this. Hobbes thought that the best way to achieve order was to have a monarch (king or queen) in control, preferably one with absolute power—complete authority with no constraints (see right). When people made an

The people are tired of fighting and seek the protection of a ruler.

Life without a ruler is brutal and warlike.

JARGON BUSTER

Authoritarian A system of government in which all the power is in the hands of a single person or small group.

State The political organization of society, including the institutions of government and the law.

Rights Moral and legal entitlements, such as food, shelter, and equal treatment.

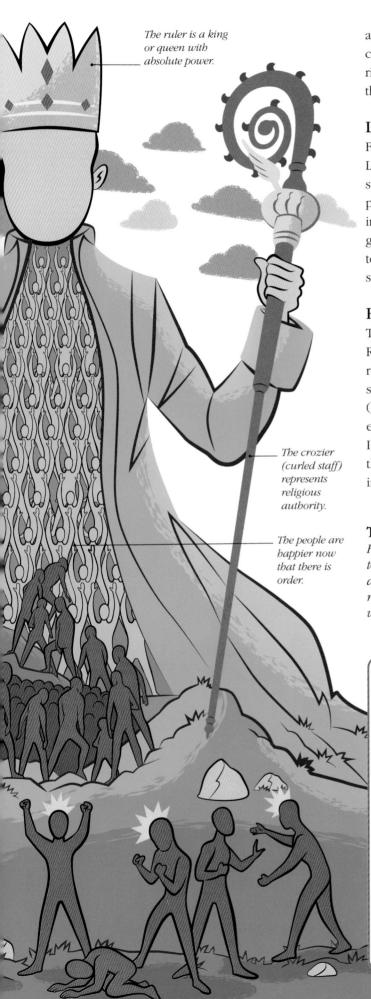

The ruler is a king or queen with absolute power.

The crozier (curled staff) represents religious authority.

The people are happier now that there is order.

agreement between themselves and the state, what he called the "social contract" (see p.161), all personal rights would be given up—except their right to protect themselves from harm.

LIMITED GOVERNMENT

For another 17th-century English philosopher, John Locke, the social contract allowed the ruling power to stay in place only for as long as it behaved well. Locke preferred the idea of "limited government"—an institution with power over only certain things. The government could just do what it was legally entitled to do, and people had rights that they didn't surrender—including, importantly, the right to rebel.

RULE BY THE PEOPLE

The 17th-century French philosopher Jean-Jacques Rousseau also placed a high priority on retaining rights, and asked how people could be governed and still remain as free as they were in the "state of nature" (see p.160). He thought this could be achieved if everyone participated in the decision-making process. In his vision, the people themselves would constitute the state, and this would prevent the state from allowing inequality to develop.

THE LEVIATHAN

Hobbes thought the best way to maintain order was to have a monarch who had absolute power—a "Leviathan." People would sacrifice most of their rights, but would be happier because their lives would be less "nasty, brutish, and short."

TYPES OF DEMOCRACY

Most of the world's states are democracies, which means that the people have a say in how they are governed. There are two principal forms of democracy: indirect and direct. Indirect democracy is a system in which the people elect others, usually professional politicians, to make decisions on their behalf. A direct democracy is one in which all the people make decisions, bypassing the role of politicians. They do this by voting in referenda.

Voting in Switzerland

165

Vandalism or self-expression?

▲ IS IT RESPECTFUL?

Hegel's ideal state is one that encourages people to behave respectfully toward one another. Graffiti can be seen as disrespectful damage to public property, but shouldn't it also be recognized as a valid form of expression?

GUARANTEES AND EXPECTATIONS

G.W.F. Hegel, a 19th-century German philosopher, thought that the state was the highest form of human organization, a combination of the moral life of the family and the freedom of civil society (the institutions that exist outside of the family and the state, such as religious groups and charities). We can see Hegel's point in political systems around the world today. The state guarantees a framework of basic human freedoms: the right to vote, civil liberties, education, and so on, while also acting as a provider of essential services, such as transportation. It lays down moral expectations too: we are encouraged to respect each other's views and not to behave in an antisocial manner.

THE STATE AS OPPRESSOR

Another 19th-century German thinker, Karl Marx, took the polar opposite view. He regarded the state as an instrument of capitalism (an economic and political system in which business is controlled by private owners for profit). He thought that the state was composed of members of this ruling class (the bourgeoisie), and that

PYRAMID OF CAPITALISM

Marx saw capitalism as a system that oppresses the working class—this is sometimes shown as a pyramid. At the top is the need to make money (capital). Beneath are various layers of power, while the workers at the bottom are being crushed.

Capitalism is driven by the need to earn money.

We **RULE** you!

Those in power demand obedience.

We **FOOL** you!

Religion persuades people that they have no choice.

The workers are tired of holding the system up.

they made decisions with their own interests in mind. This resulted in the oppression of the people (the proletariat) who worked for them. Marx predicted that capitalism would be overthrown, and that, after this, the state would no longer be needed, and would "wither away" over time (see p.175).

ABOLISHING THE STATE

Marx was an anarchist—someone who rejects the state and its intrusion into people's lives. In taking this view, he was part of a long tradition stretching back to Laozi in China, in the 6th century BCE. Some anarchist thinkers draw inspiration from both Marx and Rousseau, believing that the state should be abolished because it promotes an unequal society. Once abolished, inequalities will naturally vanish. Not all anarchists agree with them, however. Other types of anarchist, sometimes called libertarians, aren't as preoccupied with social equality. They simply regard the state's role as illegitimate (without a legal basis). In their view, nothing permits the government to intrude into people's lives unless the people have specifically allowed it. In his book *Anarchy, State and Utopia* (1974), the 20th-century American philosopher Robert Nozick made a similar point to Locke's, arguing that people have inalienable rights (rights that cannot be taken away) and that the only legitimate state is one that confines itself to protecting rights to life, liberty, and property.

We use **FORCE** against you!

The military are there to suppress any protest.

We **EAT** for you!

The businesspeople have plenty of money and food.

We **WORK** for and **FEED** **EVERYONE!**

If the workers rebel, the whole pyramid will fall.

Individuals have **rights** and there are things **no person or group** may do to them...

ROBERT NOZICK, *Anarchy, State and Utopia* (1974)

THINK FOR YOURSELF

Imagine you and your friends are stranded on a desert island. Without anyone to tell you what to do, how would you go about organizing things? You might start by making decisions together on how to divide up tasks such as finding food and building a shelter. But consider how you might settle a dispute about whether one person has done less work than another. Would it be easier if there was a leader to decide what should be done?

How should rulers behave?

Machiavelli claimed that successful rulers need to have the strength of a lion and the cunning of a fox.

Throughout history, philosophers have debated how a ruler should behave in order to keep their position. As political systems changed over time, people's expectations about how their rulers should act changed, too. Philosophers started to think less about how rulers could maintain their power and instead focused on the obligations that rulers had to their subjects.

In early history, individual rulers had an important role, as the state was not yet fully developed. Thinkers at this time discussed what an ideal ruler might be. The 5th-century Chinese philosopher Confucius believed it was the responsibility of a ruler to set an example to their people on how to live a good life (see p.122). He argued that a ruler should govern with a sense of virtue. Doing so would earn the ruler the obedience, loyalty, and respect of the people. Confucius came up with an analogy to explain his point, comparing the influence of a ruler to the power of the wind: "The moral character of the ruler is the wind; the moral character of those beneath them is the grass. When the wind blows, the grass bends."

LEADING BY EXAMPLE

Confucius thought a ruler should live a good life, setting a moral example for the people to follow. Just as the grass bends when the wind blows, the people will follow the ruler in living a good life.

The people will **obey a ruler** who behaves according to **high moral standards**. Confucius thought people should show **respect** toward their rulers.

The **grass** represents the moral character of the **people**, who are **influenced** by their ruler. Confucius said **looking up to a ruler** shows humility.

RUTHLESS LEADERSHIP

Like Confucius, the 16th-century Italian diplomat Niccolò Machiavelli talked in terms of virtue, but he used the word in a very different way. For Machiavelli, the Italian word *virtù* was a set of qualities or values that included bravery, prowess, and pride, as well as a willingness to act ruthlessly or cruelly if necessary in order to achieve an outcome.

Machiavelli is famous for the idea that the ends justify the means. In his view, all kinds of tactics, such as deception, fraud, and violence, were acceptable if the end result achieved an important goal. For Machiavelli, a ruler should behave in whatever way is necessary to maintain power. He felt that rulers are therefore justified in using any method, no matter how dishonest or unfair, to achieve their aims.

Writing in the 1600s, the English philosopher Thomas Hobbes argued similarly that it didn't matter how a ruler behaved—in effect, they could do whatever they wanted. For him, no matter how unjust or brutal a ruler was, the chaos, disorder, and loneliness that would exist in a world without a ruler would be so much worse (see p.160).

DEMOCRATIC RULE

In the 1700s, with the growth of democracies and democratic thinking (see p.165), philosophers began to consider how people could be protected from rulers who misuse their power. In his book *The Spirit of the Law* (1748), the French thinker Baron de Montesquieu argued for the separation of the powers of the state (executive, legislative, judiciary). Each part would be independent, and able to keep watch on the others. Such a division would prevent any individual part from having too much power, and using it wrongly.

Philosophers also started to think about how policy should be decided. The English philosopher Jeremy Bentham argued that governments should act according to the Principle of Utility (see p.130). He defined the right decision as the one that creates the greatest happiness of the greatest number.

◄ **PLEASURE OR PAIN?**

When making decisions, Bentham argued that a government should consider all the pleasure caused by a particular policy against all the pain. If there was more pleasure than pain, the government should carry out the policy.

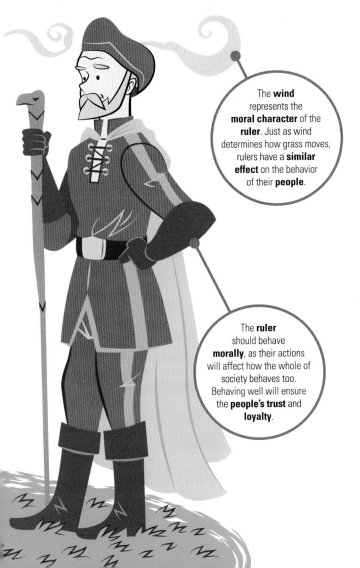

The **wind** represents the **moral character** of the **ruler**. Just as wind determines how grass moves, rulers have a **similar effect** on the behavior of their **people**.

The **ruler** should behave **morally**, as their actions will affect how the whole of society behaves too. Behaving well will ensure the **people's trust** and **loyalty**.

NICCOLÒ MACHIAVELLI

Niccolò Machiavelli (1469–1527) was an Italian diplomat and philosopher. As a high-ranking government official, he advised Lorenzo de Medici, ruler of the Florentine Republic (in present-day Italy), on how best to govern his citizens. In his most famous book, *The Prince*, published in 1532 after his death, Machiavelli set out his belief that it is better for rulers to be feared than loved, and that they should be prepared to be ruthless in pursuit of their goals.

GOVERNMENT EXAMS
The teachings of Confucius became the basis of the civil service examinations in China. Those who wished to work in the government had to prove their knowledge of Confucian texts.

Learning without **reflection** is a waste; **reflecting** without **learning** is **dangerous.**

Confucius

CHINA'S "FIRST TEACHER"

The teachings of Confucius have had a lasting impact on Chinese society, shaping the belief system that is known as Confucianism. An influential philosopher and politician, Confucius became widely known for his principles of moral behavior and his passion for education.

Confucius was born in 551 BCE in present-day Qufu, China. His given name was Kong Qui, although he later earned the title Kong Fuzi, or Confucius, meaning "Master Kong." His father died when Confucius was three years old, leaving the boy to be raised by his mother. She was his first teacher, and he was an eager student. He later studied the six traditional arts: ritual, archery, calligraphy, charioteering, arithmetic, and music. His mother died when he was 17, and this affected him deeply. Following the religious custom of the time, he spent the next three years in mourning.

THE ENCOURAGING TEACHER

An inspirational teacher, Confucius wanted education to be available to everyone, not just to the wealthy. He also believed that people should be rewarded based on their talents and hard work, not according to what family they were born into. Personal morality and respect for family relationships were key to Confucius's vision of society, and he wanted these principles to apply to government, too. Confucius worked his way up in the civil service to become Minister of Justice and tried to put his ideas into practice. However, he gave up this position at the age of 51 so that he could spread his ideas more widely by traveling around China. Some of his followers wrote down his teachings in what would later be called *The Analects of Confucius*.

Confucius died in 479 BCE. During the Western Han Dynasty (which began at the end of the 3rd century BCE), Confucius's philosophy became the main model for Chinese government and society. At different times in history, Confucius has been revered so much that he has been worshipped as a god.

SOCIETY

Rules for thinking and **living** should include following rituals, respect for elders, and self-discipline (see p.122).

A ruler should **lead by example, be humble**, and treat their followers with **compassion** (see pp.168–169).

Teachers must not preach to their students, but should instead **motivate and encourage them** in their learning.

The **five basic relationships** (*wu-lun*) are between ruler and subject, parent and child, spouses, elder and younger siblings, and friends.

What is individual freedom?

It is generally agreed that freedom is a good thing. As a concept, freedom includes things such as rights and liberties—principles that have been fought for all over the world for centuries. But is freedom something we should always aim for, and should there ever be limits to freedom?

The guarantee of freedom for every person features in the laws and principles of nearly all societies. Sometimes it appears in a special document, such as the United States Bill of Rights (1791), or the European Convention on Human Rights (1953). But what is it that people actually mean when they talk about freedom?

IMPORTANT FREEDOMS

Historically, the most important freedoms related to religion and speech. The freedom to practice a religion of your choice is protected by the US Constitution's First Amendment (1791). Freedom of speech is a right in many countries—you're able to say what you want, as long as you don't encourage hatred or violence, or wrongly attack someone's reputation. Other core freedoms include the right to protest, and to form groups such as trade unions or political parties.

LIMITS TO FREEDOM

People began to insist on these freedoms in the 18th and 19th centuries, but many of those in power were worried about freedoms going so far that society would be beyond their control. English philosopher John Stuart Mill addressed the struggle

THE IDEAS MARKET
This market is full of people explaining their ideas. J.S. Mill felt that allowing different ideas to be expressed means the best ones will attract the support of more people. He felt this would allow the truth to emerge.

between authority and freedom in his famous essay *On Liberty* (1859). He argued that governments need to be constrained by the liberty of their peoples. This means that the people must, for example, have the freedom to protest against laws they feel are unfair. He also maintained that the only reason an individual's freedom should be limited is to prevent other people from being hurt—this is Mill's Principle of Harm.

ALL VIEWS SHOULD BE HEARD

Mill went further by saying that, apart from the Principle of Harm, restrictions on speech are never justified: all points of view should be allowed, even if they offend people. (He saw offense as different from actual harm.) Different ideas need to compete with one another, just like goods in a market, where a selection to choose from allows us to buy the best products. In Mill's market, the better ideas will be supported by more people. This assumes that the views are expressed fairly and that the people who support them are acting rationally—and maybe they are not.

THE PRINCIPLE OF HARM ▶
J.S. Mill's Principle of Harm is sometimes expressed in the phrase, "My freedom to punch stops just at the end of your nose." Our own freedom must be restricted at the point where it harms others.

MARKETPLACE OF IDEAS

This idea is **not very popular** with the people at the market, but the "seller" still has the right to **express her view,** even if it offends people.

Many people like this idea. This may mean it is the **"best,"** as long as the view is expressed **fairly** and people are acting **rationally.**

FREEDOM TO AND FREEDOM FROM

Writing in the 1900s, British philosopher Isaiah Berlin argued that too much liberty is not always a good thing. He made a distinction between positive and negative freedoms. For him, positive freedom is a freedom *to do* certain things, such as practice a religion. Negative freedom is a freedom *from* things such as government interference.

Berlin felt that having too much negative freedom could lead to exploitation under the economic system of capitalism (see pp.166–167), in which certain people in society become rich at the expense of the poorer people. He described this in a memorable phrase: "Freedom for the pike is death for the minnow."

Berlin highlighted a conflict between positive and negative freedoms: in order for some people to be free to pursue their own goals, restrictions must be placed on the more powerful. In his view, this shows there must be a limit to the freedoms given to the people.

PIKE AND MINNOW ▶
Isaiah Berlin described the possible effects of unlimited negative freedom in an analogy. Powerful people (represented by a pike) could dominate weaker ones (a minnow).

The large, aggressive pike can easily swallow the tiny minnow.

How can societies be changed?

Throughout history, political thinkers have debated how to improve society. Some believe that society should stay largely as it is, with any necessary changes evolving gradually over time. Others think, for all sorts of reasons, that society must change and that this should come about through revolution—a complete overthrow of the system.

At the end of the 1700s, France had a revolution— a period of social, political, and economic upheaval that resulted in the overthrow of the monarchy and suppression of the Catholic Church. This time of change led Irish-born philosopher Edmund Burke and English-born writer Thomas Paine to engage in a now-famous debate about whether gradual change or revolution was the best way to transform society.

Burke was critical of the French Revolution, arguing that all dramatic change was dangerous, and could have unintended consequences. For him, society was held together by traditional institutions such as monarchy and religion. Burke thought that people were attached to these institutions, and destroying them would endanger society. He saw revolution as a backward step; he wasn't against change, but he believed that it should happen gradually.

Sometimes, large changes can be made from above.

CHANGE FROM ABOVE
The building is being modified gradually, under the control of those who own it. However, this process does not guarantee that the building will be preserved forever.

Small changes don't really alter the nature of the building.

The building's owners direct the changes happening above.

CHANGE FROM BELOW
These workers feel that the changes made from above are not far-reaching enough. They want to replace the building entirely, and so are trying to bring it down from below ground.

Workers chip away at the foundations

174

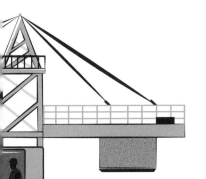

Paine wrote that… **each generation** should be free to have the political **system it wants**, not one from the past.

TWO TYPES OF CHANGE

Revolutions can come from above, directed by the ruling class, or from below, as a result of action by the working class. We can think of this in terms of making changes to a building. The changes made from above happen in a controlled way, while the actions below are less precise.

In contrast, Paine was a supporter of the revolution in France, believing that the French monarchy was incapable of gradual reform. He wrote in the *Rights of Man* (1791) that each generation controls its own political destiny and should be free to have the political system it wants, not be left with one from the past. Paine thought that giving too much importance to preserving traditional institutions was like giving dead people votes.

REVOLUTION FROM BELOW

Like Paine, the 19th-century German thinker Karl Marx was enthusiastic about revolution. Influenced by G.W.F. Hegel's theory of the dialectic (see p.27), Marx saw revolution as inevitable, governed by the laws of history.

He was writing during the Industrial Age—a time of widespread unrest in Europe. For him, revolution would come from below, with the exploited working class (proletariat) seeking to overthrow the capitalist system (see p.166) and take power themselves. The working class would eventually create a classless society where ownership of business was shared among all people—a system called communism. Because the bourgeoisie (wealthy business owners) would strongly defend their privileged position under capitalism, Marx believed only revolution from below could achieve radical change.

REVOLUTION FROM ABOVE

At the same time, another theory about how societies could change emerged—the idea of revolution from above. This is a situation in which the ruling power itself introduces dramatic social, political, and economic changes, but in a controlled way. It might do this in order to limit discontent among the people and therefore avoid revolution from below, allowing it to preserve its dominant position in society.

◀ MARX'S THEORY
Marx was influenced by Hegel's theory of the dialectic, in which opposing forces and ideas clash, and a new and better system is produced. Marx thought that the working class would overthrow the bourgeoisie, resulting in an equal and fair communist society.

Karl Marx

SOCIALIST REVOLUTIONARY

Famous for his criticism of the wealthy and powerful, Karl Marx was a philosopher, economist, and political activist. His views on the class struggle between the rich and poor led to Marx calling for drastic political change to create a more equal society.

Marx was born in Trier, Prussia (now in modern-day Germany) in 1818. He was the son of Heinrich Marx, a successful Jewish lawyer, and Henriette Pressburg. The family converted to Lutheranism (a branch of Christianity) when Marx was six, but as a child he nevertheless experienced discrimination for his Jewish heritage. He briefly studied law in 1835 in Bonn, where he was imprisoned for rebellious behavior. He enrolled at the University of Berlin in 1836, where he became involved with the "Young Hegelians," a group of activists who argued for social reform based on the theories of G.W.F. Hegel (see p.27).

SOCIAL DIVIDE

Marx became a journalist in 1842, but was forced to leave Prussia for his radical writing. He went to Paris in 1843, where he met Friedrich Engels. This wealthy writer supported Marx financially, allowing him to continue his work. In 1845 Marx was once again exiled, this time settling in Brussels with Engels, where together they wrote *The Communist Manifesto* (1848). This book outlined their ideas on how the society of the time would eventually be replaced by socialism, a political system in which the government owns businesses and shares the profits equally between all citizens.

Political unrest in Europe during 1848 led to one final move, this time to England. Here Marx wrote *Capital* (1867), one of the most influential books of the 1800s. In it, he analyzed the economic system of capitalism, where wealth (capital) is generated for private business owners, rather than for the state, by the labor of others. Marx died in London in 1883, unaware that his theories would play a significant role in communist revolutions all over the world in the following century.

The aim of **capitalism** is to create wealth. It is unequal and **unjust** because it **exploits the proletariat** (working class), which does not receive a share of the profits (see pp.166–167).

Once the **proletariat** understands its situation, it will **overthrow the bourgeoisie** (business owners). After the revolution, the proletariat will temporarily run the state.

The **material conditions** of the world, such as the economic system and the **distribution of wealth**, help explain the relationship between the different classes in society.

Eventually, the state will cease to exist, leading to a **communist society**, where businesses are owned by the people and **profits are shared equally** (see p.175).

RUSSIAN REVOLUTION
Marx's socialist theory inspired the Russian Revolution of 1917. Workers and soldiers became dissatisfied with the behavior of the Tsar and the corrupt government, so they worked together to overthrow them.

The **history** of all hitherto existing **society** is the history of **class struggles**.

How can we ensure equality?

An equal society is one in which every citizen has the same rights, regardless of their sex, gender, race, sexuality, physical and intellectual abilities, and economic and social position. Today, almost all philosophers agree that everybody deserves equal rights, but the question of equal treatment in practice is more controversial.

Equality is an important contemporary political issue, but it is quite a recent concern among philosophers. One of the earliest philosophical debates about equality centered on the issue of equal rights for women.

WOMEN'S EQUALITY

Philosophers began to campaign for women to be considered equal to men in the 1700s. For French philosopher Olympe de Gouges, rights were natural and everybody was entitled to them, regardless of their sex. Writing during the French Revolution (1789–1799), de Gouges was critical of the *Declaration of the Rights of Man and of the Citizen* (1789), a civil rights document that supposedly gave equal rights to all citizens but referred only to men. Her response was to publish the *Declaration of the Rights of Woman and of the Citizen* in 1791, which argued for the rights of women to speak freely, to be educated, to own property, and to vote.

In 1792 the English writer Mary Wollstonecraft challenged the widespread belief held at the time that women were inferior to men. Wollstonecraft imagined a more equal society, arguing that women had just as much potential as men, but their lack of access to education made it seem as if they were less capable. She believed that educating women would allow them to make a bigger contribution to society.

In *The Second Sex* (1949), French philosopher Simone de Beauvoir outlined how, historically, society has defined women only in relation to men. De Beauvoir thought that women are judged for their differences from men, who are held up by society as an idealized standard. She described how men are seen as

"the subject" and women as "the other." For de Beauvoir, women could free themselves from this "othering" by recognizing that gender—the roles and characteristics that are typically given to women and men—is socially constructed, and not a natural or inherent part of being female or male.

EQUALITY OF OPPORTUNITY
All three people have the same opportunity to see the game by using a crate. However, their starting points are not the same, so the wheelchair-user still can't see over the wall.

This person is tall enough to see, with or without a crate.

The child can see over the wall with the aid of the crate.

The wheelchair user can't use a crate, so he can't see the game.

EXTENDING EQUAL RIGHTS

This "othering" also happens in relation to racial difference, and to differences in culture, physical and intellectual abilities, and sexuality—in fact, to anyone who differs from the norm established by any particular society. Many philosophers have addressed the issue of racial inequality, and contemporary thinkers are also analyzing the notion of difference with regards to sexuality and ability. The 20th-century American philosopher Richard Rorty, for example, suggested that we try to expand our sense of "us" as much as possible in order to reduce "othering." This means that when we meet people we instinctively think of as different, i.e. people who we might call "them" rather than "us," we should try to find similarities between us, rather than focusing on any differences.

ECONOMIC EQUALITY

There are no good arguments for inequality based on sex, gender, race, sexuality, and ability, but the issue of economic equality is more controversial. When thinking about economic equality, philosophers distinguish between equality of outcome and equality of

THINK FOR YOURSELF

It's your birthday and you're having a party with all your friends. Your parents ask you to cut up your birthday cake so that they can hand it round to everyone. You don't know which slice will go to whom, including yourself. Which way of cutting the cake (shown below) would you choose? Is it worth the risk to cut a large slice, hoping you get it, but knowing that you could also end up with the smallest slice?

opportunity (see illustration left). In a society where the equality of outcome is preferred, every person should end up with the same amount of wealth, regardless of their starting point. This is what the 19th-century German thinker Karl Marx was aiming for: a classless society where wealth was redistributed evenly among the people (see p.175). However, some philosophers think that this would reduce people's motivation to work. The idea of equality of opportunity involves a different approach. It relies on the same opportunities being available for all, regardless of social or economic position, in order to encourage motivation and competition among people.

In 1971 American philosopher John Rawls changed the debate by asking people to consider how to achieve a *just* outcome rather than an *equal* one. Rawls wondered how people would share a sum of money among a group if they didn't know how much they would receive themselves. He argued that not knowing would make people more inclined to ensure that the money was evenly distributed—for Rawls, this is what is meant by fairness. This approach—putting people behind a "veil of ignorance"—is a way for decision-makers to judge whether economic and social policies really are fair for everyone.

EQUALITY OF OUTCOME
Not everyone has a crate, and the wheelchair-user has additional things so that he can see over the wall. However, the outcome is the same for all three: they can watch the game.

This person can see over the wall without a crate.

The result for the child is the same, but this time his needs have been considered.

To see over the wall safely, the wheelchair-user needs two crates and a ramp.

THE EQUALITY GAME
This family doesn't have tickets for the game, so is trying to watch it by looking over a wall. The two scenarios show the difference between equality of opportunity (each having a crate to use) and equality of outcome (having what each of them needs to see the game).

Mary Wollstonecraft

PIONEERING WRITER ABOUT WOMEN'S RIGHTS

An inspirational writer and thinker who was ahead of her time, Mary Wollstonecraft dedicated her short life to the improvement of women's rights and to the promotion of free education for everybody. She is regarded as one of the earliest feminist philosophers.

Born in 1759 in London, England, Wollstonecraft had an abusive father, which caused her to leave home after the death of her mother in 1780. At the age of 24, she set up a small school for girls with her two sisters and a friend. Although it closed after a year, it helped to frame her ideas on female education.

In 1786 Wollstonecraft briefly went to be a governess (teacher) in Ireland. On her return to London, she met a group of liberal thinkers, including radical publisher Joseph Johnson, who published her first book, *Thoughts on the Education of Daughters* (1787). Her work suggested that the education system should be reformed so that girls could receive the same education as boys.

Wollstonecraft's most important work, *A Vindication of the Rights of Woman* (1792), was written at a time when women in Britain either worked in poorly paid jobs or were expected to stay at home being wives and mothers. She argued that both women and men had equal rights to freedom and education, and that women should have the right to vote so that they could contribute more fully to society.

FINDING HAPPINESS

After Wollstonecraft gave birth to a daughter in 1794, she had long periods of depression. Eventually, she found happiness with the unconventional political philosopher William Godwin. Despite being against marriage because it limited freedom, she married Godwin because she was pregnant with his child. She had another daughter in 1797, named Mary, who went on to write the famous Gothic novel *Frankenstein*. Sadly, Wollstonecraft did not survive the birth.

It took until the mid-1800s for Wollstonecraft's radical ideas on women's rights to be taken up by women's movements in Europe and the US. Today she is regarded as the founder of liberal feminism.

Women may be physically weaker than men, but they are just as **capable of rational thought.**

The **mind** has **no gender**: girls should be taught in the **same schools** as boys, and given the same job opportunities.

Women only **appear** to be **inferior** because they do not receive the **same standard of education** as men (see p.178).

Women must be defined by their **character**, and not by who they marry. An ideal marriage should be based on **mutual respect** and **intellectual companionship**.

EDUCATING GIRLS
Wollstonecraft's passionate ideas and political writings helped promote female education as a basic right in most areas of the world. These Sudanese girls are living in a refugee camp, but are continuing with their education in this school.

I do not wish them [women] to have **power over men**; but over **themselves**.

FEMINIST PHILOSOPHY

For many years feminist philosophers have analyzed the inequalities that exist between men and women, and have criticized systems where males have all the power (patriarchies). Their work has helped to create increasingly fairer societies, where men and women are given equal rights to study, debate, and vote.

"Reserve your right to think, for even to think wrongly is better than not to think at all."

◄ HYPATIA
(360–415 CE)
From Alexandria in Egypt, Hypatia was a mathematician and astronomer as well as a philosopher. As the only woman of her time to study and teach these subjects, she is now seen as a feminist icon.

▼ INÉS DE LA CRUZ (1648–1695)
Mexican nun and thinker de la Cruz criticized women's limited access to education during the 1600s, and stated that there was nothing in Christianity that prevented the education of women.

"If all Men are born free, how is it that all Women are born slaves?"

▲ MARY ASTELL (1666–1731)
A feminist pioneer, English philosopher Astell stated that a wife must be treated as an equal by her husband in order to have a happy marriage.

"Who has forbidden women to engage in private and individual studies? Have they not a rational soul as men do?"

OLYMPE DE GOUGES ▶
(1748–1793)
French writer de Gouges argued that since women were treated equally to men with regard to the death penalty, their opinions should also be considered equally.

"A woman has the right to be guillotined; she should also have the right to debate."

"How grossly do they insult us, who thus advise us only to render ourselves gentle, domestic brutes!"

◄ MARY WOLLSTONECRAFT (1759–1797)
English writer and philosopher Wollstonecraft passionately criticized the educational system of her time, which she believed undermined the intelligence of women, and limited their opportunities.

▼ HARRIET TAYLOR MILL (1807–1858)
British thinker Mill co-authored many of her husband J.S. Mill's books. She argued for a woman's right to vote, and sought gender-equal access to jobs.

"One is not born, but rather becomes, a woman."

SIMONE DE BEAUVOIR (1908–1986) ▲
French existentialist de Beauvoir explained that men and women are born equal, but society shapes women to become inferior to men.

"Numbers of women are wives and mothers only because there is no other career open to them."

"God's plan is often a front for men's plans, and a cover for inadequacy, ignorance, and evil."

MARY DALY ▶ (1928–2010)
American feminist and theologian Daly criticized some religions for giving men a reason to treat women unfairly.

"We must learn to speak the language women speak when there is no one there to correct us."

◄ HÉLÈNE CIXOUS (born 1937)
Algerian-French philosopher Cixous pioneered a unique form of writing known as écriture feminine ("women's writing") to explore the struggle for identity in a world where women are defined by men.

"Most cultures have as one of their principal aims the control of women by men."

▲ SUSAN MOLLER OKIN (1946–2004)
New Zealand-born Okin was a leading feminist political theorist—she was interested in identifying gender inequalities in political philosophy and society.

BEAUTY AND ART

The philosophy of beauty and art is called aesthetics. Many philosophers have tried to define beauty, and have asked if we all find the same kinds of things beautiful. They have also explored whether it is ever right to censor artists and their work. In the 20th century, philosophers turned their attention to finding a common quality that unites all works of art.

What is beauty?

We all recognize beauty when we see it, but it can be difficult to say exactly what beauty is, and why it matters to us. Philosophers have offered a number of different ways to understand beauty. One central issue is whether our perception of beauty is subjective (something that is a matter of individual taste), or whether it's universal (something everyone can agree on).

In Western philosophy, the subject of beauty and how it's represented in art dates back to the ancient Greeks, when Plato discussed it in his written dialogues (conversations). Thinkers came to the topic again in the early 1700s; at this time the philosophical study of beauty and art became known as "aesthetics."

BEAUTY AND LOVE

The ancient Greek philosopher Plato thought that the appreciation of beauty can lead us to moral goodness. In Plato's book the *Symposium* (c.385–370 bce), the character Socrates (based on Plato's real-life teacher) discusses the nature of love with other guests at a party. Socrates relates the priestess Diotima's theory of love. According to Diotima, when we love a person, what we love is their beauty. We then move from loving one beautiful individual to recognizing beauty in others. After this, we move in stages, learning to love other types of beauty, such as the beauty of other people's minds, and the beauty found in all types of knowledge. Finally, we love the Form of the Good itself—the source of all beauty. The Good includes not just the concept of beauty, but also moral goodness.

DIOTIMA'S LADDER

Plato's theory of beauty is based on the teachings of the priestess Diotima. According to her, appreciating beauty is like climbing the rungs of a ladder. We begin with loving the beauty of a single person. From there, we move in steps, learning to love beauty in others, until we recognize the source of all beauty: the Form of the Good.

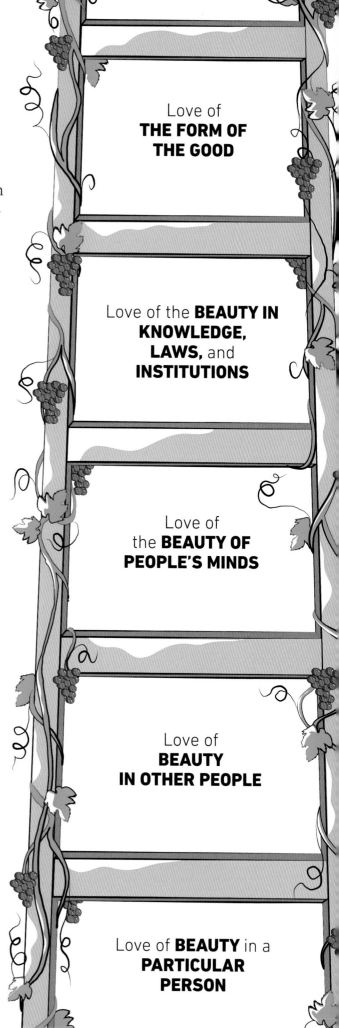

Love of
**THE FORM OF
THE GOOD**

Love of the **BEAUTY IN
KNOWLEDGE,
LAWS,** and
INSTITUTIONS

Love of
the **BEAUTY OF
PEOPLE'S MINDS**

Love of
**BEAUTY
IN OTHER PEOPLE**

Love of **BEAUTY** in a
**PARTICULAR
PERSON**

Plato thought that the appreciation of beauty can lead us to moral goodness.

For Plato, true beauty, like all concepts, only exists in the heavenly world of Forms (see pp.52–53). Beauty is an ideal, and any particular beautiful person or thing in the real world is, by definition, an imperfect copy of the Form. Few people accept this now, but Plato's ideas on beauty have had a huge impact, not just on philosophy, but on the visual arts. For example, some artists of the Renaissance period (14th–17th centuries) attempted to paint idealized beauty, rather than depicting people as they really were.

A TYPE OF FEAR

In his aesthetic theory, the 18th-century Irish-born philosopher Edmund Burke analyzed beauty partly by contrasting it with another aesthetic term, the "sublime" (the quality of greatness). Burke stated that beautiful objects tend to be small and intricate, whereas sublime things, such as towering mountains and rushing waterfalls, are large and terrifying. Beautiful things can produce a certain kind of pleasure, but sublime objects give us a stronger emotional reaction that comes from our awareness of their potential danger. This means that our idea of beauty is partly related to feelings of fear and terror—we appreciate sublime things *because* there is an element of threat.

FROM THE PERSONAL TO THE UNIVERSAL

The 18th-century German philosopher Immanuel Kant analyzed the subject of beauty in his *Critique of the Power of Judgement* (1790). He wrote that people make judgments about beauty based on their feelings, particularly the feeling of pleasure. This pleasure is "disinterested," which means that we find something pleasurable because we consider it to be

▲ THE SUBLIME IN ART
Poets and painters of the 18th-century Romantic Movement were particularly interested in the idea of the sublime, and often wrote about or painted gloomy and threatening landscapes.

beautiful, rather than thinking it beautiful because it gives us pleasure. However, our judgments about beauty are never just personal: we think everyone else should have the same reaction, too—there is a *universal* element to our opinion. However, for Kant, there are no general laws about which things are beautiful. For example, you can't say that every landscape painting is beautiful just because the one that you're looking at is. You can only make a judgment on that particular painting, but when you do this, you are doing something more than simply expressing your personal view.

MOVING AWAY FROM TRADITION

For Kant, beauty was key to understanding works of art. However, in the early 1900s, many artists working in the West started to move away from trying to create what most people considered to be beautiful. Some

A beautiful rose

Are all red flowers beautiful?

◀ NO GENERAL LAWS
According to Kant's theory, we can't say that all red flowers are beautiful just because the red rose in front of us is. Instead, we have to experience each particular flower and make a judgment on a case-by-case basis.

deliberately made works that were "anti-aesthetic," i.e. lacked beauty. Other artistic qualities, such as originality, were more important to them. The French-American artist Marcel Duchamp was famous for a work called *Fountain* (1917)—a porcelain urinal that had been made in a factory. He submitted it to an art society for exhibition in New York, unchanged aside from the addition of a signature. He did this to challenge the art world's preconceptions of beauty and what made something a work of art. It was rejected by the society's committee, which Duchamp regarded as an act of censorship.

◄ **THE URINAL**
Duchamp's Fountain, *a ready-made urinal, wasn't considered a work of art in 1917, but has inspired artists ever since. Duchamp signed it "R. Mutt" so that he could remain anonymous.*

BEAUTY IN IMPERFECTION

Most theories about beauty, like Plato's, suggest a kind of ideal, and emphasize perfection. This isn't true of every culture. The ancient Japanese concept of *wabi-sabi* finds beauty in the damaged, the imperfect, the incomplete, and the impermanent. It acknowledges that the attempt to make life perfect is the main cause of our frustration and unhappiness. The philosophy of *wabi-sabi* incorporates seven principles: *kanso* (simplicity), fukinsei (irregular forms and shapes), shibumi (beauty in simplicity), *shizen* (the inclusion of nature), *yugen* (subtle beauty), datsuzoku (being spontaneous), and *seijaku* (tranquility and calm). These are present in many parts of Japanese artistic life, such as music composition, garden design, and the creation of *kintsugi* pottery (see box).

Hmm… **COZY**, and **PLENTY** of **FOOD** and **WATER** nearby as well.

Trees provide firewood.

Animals can be hunted for food.

Water is essential for survival.

THE ART INSTINCT

In the 1900s, some thinkers, including American philosopher Denis Dutton, noted that there is so much agreement about what is beautiful, and claimed that there must be an explanation based on evolution for this. In the Pleistocene era, commonly known as the Ice Age, human beings could only survive where there was shelter, food, and water. Finding such places was a matter of life and death. Dutton argued that when we

THE ART OF *KINTSUGI*

The Japanese art of *kintsugi*, which translates as "golden joinery," is the technique of mending broken pottery with gold or lacquer to draw attention to the repaired cracks that others might see as defects. This practice, which dates back to about the 1400s, embraces the Japanese philosophy of *wabi-sabi*, which appreciates imperfections as beauty, and highlights the "scars" instead of covering them up. It also emphasizes the idea of recycling: if something is broken it can be fixed and reused.

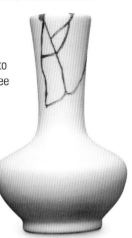

***Kintsugi* vase**

And this fantastic cave comes with **CENTRAL HEATING** and **DECOR** of the highest quality. You won't find better!

look at water, trees, and hills where caves may be, we feel a sense of comfort, subconsciously connecting these features with our most basic human instinct of survival. According to Dutton, we call art that represents this sort of landscape "beautiful" because it shows the kind of place that would have appealed to our distant ancestors.

The cave provides shelter and protection.

AN IDEAL HOME

Dutton claimed that "beautiful" art features the things that were essential to our ancestors for survival. In our imaginary scene, a realtor from the Ice Age is explaining to a couple why this cave and its location are perfect.

FOR SALE

What is art?

What do a pile of bricks, a light going on and off, an oil painting, and a symphony have in common? The answer is that they have all been called "works of art." But what makes them so? Is it just because they can be viewed in an art gallery or listened to in a concert hall, or is there something that these things have in common that makes them "art?"

Artists—including painters, writers, musicians, and dancers—have often pushed the limits of what people think art is, and this was particularly so in the early 1900s in the West. Visual artists started working with new kinds of materials, using things such as newspapers and matchboxes, and ready-made objects such as a urinal (see p.188). Composers made music with new harmonies and using different kinds of sound, and dance broke away from the restrictive rules of classical ballet. Philosophers from the 1900s onward began to question what qualifies as art, and to see whether there was anything that could link these very diverse art forms together.

A COMMON FORM

The English art critics Clive Bell and Roger Fry claimed that all visual arts have a particular form in common that viewers can recognize. Bell called this "significant form"—lines and colors combined in a certain way. Bell and Fry argued that it doesn't matter what the works of art represent—they could even be abstract paintings, i.e. ones that don't represent things in a realistic way. What matters is that their forms produce an emotion in the viewer (e.g. sadness, wonder, awe). In their view, what makes something a work of art is its power to affect us profoundly through its use of these common forms.

ART AS SELF-EXPRESSION

The English philosopher R.G. Collingwood claimed that art was a type of self-expression. According to him, artists begin working with a vague understanding of an emotion, and come to understand precisely what they feel through creating a work of art. This is different from using art to *represent* an emotion, where an artist tries to depict, say, anger in their work. Until the emotion is expressed artistically, the artist won't really understand it: the emotion will be unclear. When somebody views, reads, or listens to the completed work, they are able to feel the artist's expressed emotion themselves, which gives them greater understanding of it (see illustration

A painted portrait

A bronze sculpture

An abstract painting

◀ **THINGS IN COMMON?**
According to Bell and Fry, all works of visual art, no matter how different they seem, share common forms that classify them as "art." These forms include lines and colors.

EXPRESSING A FEELING

Collingwood claimed that art is a process of self-discovery. The sculptor understands a particular emotion better through creating a work of art. The viewer goes through a similar process, making their emotion more precise by looking at the work.

right). Art for Collingwood was very different from craft (objects that have a function or use, such as a knitted sweater or a clay pot). In craft, the maker has a blueprint (pattern or design) and knows in advance how things will turn out—emotions need not be involved.

FAMILY RESEMBLANCE

Thinkers like Bell, Fry, and Collingwood assumed that all art must have something in common. From the 1950s onward, philosophers influenced by 20th-century Austrian thinker Ludwig Wittgenstein began to argue that there is no single feature that all works of art must share to be considered art. They used Wittgenstein's theory of "family resemblance" (see p.101) to explain that there are only *some* overlapping features between the things

191

we call art. Think of your biological relatives. You and another family member may have the same eye color; they may have different hair from you, but share that hair type with another relative. You all resemble each other, but there isn't a feature that you all have in common. This can also be applied to art. For example, many works of art represent fictional characters. However, not all works of art do that—portrait paintings depict real people, and most abstract paintings don't represent anything at all. A painted portrait is similar to an abstract painting because it's a painting; portrait paintings resemble paintings of fictional characters in some ways, but not in others. There is no *single* quality that all these different works of art share that makes them works of art.

INSTITUTIONAL THEORY

The American philosopher George Dickie suggested that the thinkers influenced by Wittgenstein's idea of "family resemblance" were wrong, and that all works of art *do* share some features, it's just that these features aren't directly visible. According to Dickie's "institutional theory,"

works of art have two things in common. First, they are all artifacts (things that have been created by someone). Second, artifacts become art by being recognized by members of the art world, such as gallery owners, art critics, publishers, or famous conductors. These powerful figures are part of an institution that defines art. They can turn more or less anything into a work of art, including an old bed, a pile of bricks, or a jumble of words or noise, just by inviting people to look at, read, or listen to them in a certain way—this is what Dickie calls making the object "a candidate for appreciation" (see illustration below). Dickie didn't think that making something a work of art by treating it in this way necessarily meant it was a "good" work of art—he considered that to be a separate question.

? WHEN IS IT ART?

Dickie claimed that things are called "art" when members of art institutions ask us to look at them in a certain way. What does this mean for the man on his way to an art gallery? He passes a pile of bricks on a building site and thinks nothing of it. But when he enters the gallery, he sees an identical pile of bricks, only this time it is "art."

The man passes a **pile of bricks** on his way to an art gallery. They are **ordinary materials** on a **building site** and he barely notices them— why would he?

THE PERFECT FORGERY

Forgeries (fakes) are an interesting challenge to any theory of art. There are two types of forgery: one that is a copy of a work that already exists and is intended to deceive the viewer, and one that is a "new" work in the style of another artist. Suppose a person manages to create a perfect copy of a painting by another artist, would the forgery be a work of art? If the two paintings are visually identical, and the original was considered a work of art, then surely the forgery must be one, too. But, as the American philosopher and art critic Arthur Danto argued, just because two objects *look* the same, it doesn't mean they have the same *properties*. Danto claimed that, aside from the moral issue of deception, which might make us disapprove of a copy, forgeries lack the creativity and expressiveness of the original work. For thinkers such as Danto, our appreciation of art doesn't just come from what it looks like, it includes what we know about the artist's intentions.

THE MASTER FORGER

The 20th-century Dutch painter Han van Meegeren painted works in the style of many grand masters, including the 17th-century artist Johannes Vermeer. These forgeries fooled the art experts of the day, and van Meegeren's paintings sold for huge sums of money. Van Meegeren was caught after World War II when he was accused of selling a genuine Vermeer to the Nazis—an act of treason. Van Meegeren confessed to the lesser crime of forgery, proving in court that he had painted the so-called Vermeer himself.

Han van Meegeren

Should art ever be censored?

A number of Western philosophers have debated the morality of art, and asked whether it serves any useful purpose. Some thinkers have claimed that art can offend people, corrupt them, or misrepresent the truth, and that it should therefore be censored (limited or suppressed). Most modern philosophers are in favor of free expression in the arts.

JARGON BUSTER

Corrupt To destroy the moral worth or correctness of something or someone.

Free expression The act of communicating our thoughts and beliefs without restrictions.

Represent To portray something in words or images.

Many artists believe in their right to express themselves freely. They think that there should be no limits on what they can represent in their work. But are they right? The ancient Greek philosopher Plato, for one, disagreed with them.

COPYING A COPY

In the *Republic* (c.375 BCE), Plato discussed how to create an ideal society (see p.164), and stated that artists wouldn't be welcome to join. For Plato, things we can see in the world are already imitations or copies of the ideal things in the world of Forms (see pp.52–53). So when we make a picture or a sculpture, we are making a copy of a copy. Since all objects in the real world are imperfect representations of what exists in the world of Forms, the artist's version of an object distorts

Art is a **great hall** of reflection where **we can all meet**…
IRIS MURDOCH, *The Fire and the Sun* (1977)

reality even further. Plato believed this led to a misunderstanding about how things really are. Therefore, he would turn artists away at the borders of his ideal republic because they misrepresented the truth.

ART REVEALS TRUTH

The 20th-century English philosopher and novelist Iris Murdoch partly agreed with Plato, saying that in our moral lives we should try to move from illusion to reality by acknowledging the Good—the Form of beauty and morality (see pp.186–187). However, unlike Plato, Murdoch argued the case for art in her book *The Fire and the Sun* (1977) by claiming that great artworks have the power to reveal beauty and truths about reality.

FREEDOM OF EXPRESSION

Many philosophers and other thinkers have argued in favor of free expression in the arts and beyond. For example, in his book *Areopagitica* (1644), the 17th-century English poet and scholar John Milton argued that books have life in them, and to censor them is almost like killing someone, and so is morally wrong. In the 1800s, the English thinker John Stuart Mill argued that people's views should be allowed to circulate freely, even if they are offensive (see pp.172–173). Otherwise, without proper debate, people may accept things

A copy   A copy of a copy

▲ **FALSE REPRESENTATION**
Plato claimed that our world is an imperfect copy of a perfect world—the world of Forms. He argued that artists distort our imperfect world even further by making a copy of something that is already a copy.

TO CENSOR OR NOT?

In this scenario, an artist is painting a portrait, expressing himself freely—but not everyone likes the result. The three art students feel differently about whether the painting should be seen by others or censored.

without thinking them through. However, if views cause actual harm, they should be censored—that's where Mill drew the line.

A CHALLENGE TO FREE EXPRESSION

The contemporary Australian-British philosopher Rae Langton challenges the idea that offensive views should always be allowed to circulate. Langton points out that speech is "doing things with words," and she claims that hate speech is more than offensive: it harms people. She also believes that some images, like speech, can hurt others. For example, false and abusive representations can be very damaging. Images and words can also be used as propaganda (selective information that promotes a specific view) that can lead to hatred and violence against certain groups in society. None of this can be easily defended on free speech grounds.

THINK FOR YOURSELF

Imagine you're at the movies with your friends. The film is enjoyable and makes you think differently about the world. However, the main character is rebellious, uses bad language, and commits crimes without facing the consequences. After this, you notice that your friends start quoting lines from the film and speaking rudely to others. But is the film itself to blame? Should it be censored to prevent this from happening?

PHILOSOPHERS ON BEAUTY AND ART

From the earliest times to the present day, philosophers all over the world have analyzed what beauty is, what art is for, and how people respond to it. This branch of philosophy is called aesthetics.

"**Art has no end but its own perfection.**"

◄ PLATO (c.429–347 BCE)
Ancient Greek philosopher Plato insisted that art does nothing more than represent what is already in the ideal world of Forms.

FRANCIS BACON (1561–1626) ▼
English philosopher Bacon stated that it is impossible to know true beauty without considering its opposite—imperfection.

▼ PLOTINUS (204–270 CE)
According to Roman philosopher Plotinus, beauty cannot arise from ugly things. For a song to be beautiful, every note must have a beauty of its own.

"**There is no excellent beauty that hath not some strangeness in the proportion.**"

"But if the whole is beautiful the parts must be beautiful too; a beautiful whole can certainly not be composed of ugly parts; all the parts must have beauty."

DAVID HUME (1711–1776) ▼
In his aesthetic theory, Scottish philosopher Hume explained that beauty is subjective, and that feeling, not thought, helps people decide whether an object is beautiful or ugly.

"Beauty is no quality in things themselves; it exists merely in the mind which contemplates them..."

Glossary

A posteriori Something that can only be known on the basis of experience.

A priori Something that can be known through *reasoning* alone, without the need of experience.

Aesthetics The *branch of philosophy* concerned with the *concept* of beauty and the principles of art.

Allegory A story that has a hidden, usually *moral*, meaning.

Analogy A comparison of one thing to another thing to help explain or clarify its meaning.

Analytic philosophy A type of thinking that examines a *theory* by taking it apart using the tools of *logic* and language.

Analytic truth A sentence that is *true* by definition, because of the meanings of the words used to express it, e.g. "A square has four equal sides." The opposite is a *synthetic truth*.

Anomaly Something that deviates from the *norm*, or that is unexpected.

Argument In philosophy, a set of sentences in which one sentence is being declared to be *true* on the basis of the others.

Artificial intelligence The intelligence demonstrated by a computer system that has been designed to perform tasks that usually require human intelligence.

Atheism The lack of *belief* in any god or gods.

Attribute A quality or feature that is an essential part of something.

Authentic In philosophy, being genuine or *true* to yourself.

Authoritarian A system of government in which all the power is in the hands of a single person or small group.

Behaviorism The study of outward behavioral signals rather than internal thoughts.

Belief An acceptance or trust that something is *true*, even when it is without evidence.

Benevolent Well-meaning, helpful, and kindly.

Bias A personal judgment that tends to favor one thing over another, often unfairly.

Branch of philosophy Area of philosophy, such as *metaphysics*, *epistemology*, *logic*, and *ethics*.

Capitalism An economic and political system in which the

working class creates wealth (capital) for private business owners (rather than the *state*).

Claim A *statement* that something is *true*.

Communism A political and economic system in which everyone belongs to the same social class, and wealth is shared equally among the people.

Concept A notion or idea.

Conclusion The final part of an *argument* that is a consequence of the argument's *premises*.

Consequentialism The view that a good act is one that brings about the best consequences, regardless of the person's intention.

Contemporary Existing or occurring at the same time; existing or occurring in the present time.

Continental philosophy European philosophy in the 19th and 20th centuries that focuses on combining different ideas together, especially to explore the nature of human experience.

Contingent Something that may or may not be the case. The opposite is *necessary*.

Contradiction A *statement* or statements containing ideas that cannot all be *true* at the same time.

Corrupt To destroy the *moral* worth or correctness of something or someone.

Deduction The method of *reasoning* from one or more *premises* to a logically *necessary conclusion*. See also *induction*.

Deontology The view that an act is good when it is done with the right intentions, regardless of the outcome of that act.

Description In *logic*, an expression that takes the form of the word "the," "a," or "an" followed by a noun group, for example, "the President of Antarctica."

Determinism The view that all events, including human actions, are the result of previous causes; an argument against *free will*.

Dialectic A method of discovering *truth* by discussing ideas with people with differing views; in the philosophy of G.W.F. Hegel, the interaction between opposing sides.

Dialogue A conversation between two or more people, sometimes used to look at different sides of a philosophical *argument*.

Dualism The view that reality is formed of two *substances*. See also *monism*, *pluralism*.

Emotivism The view that *ethical* judgments are just expressions of our emotions.

Empirical Based on what is experienced, as opposed to what can be figured out by *reasoning*.

Empiricism The view that all *knowledge* of things that exist outside the *mind* is acquired through the experiences of the senses.

Epistemology The *branch of philosophy* that explores what

knowledge is, what we can know, how we can gain knowledge, and if there are limits to what we can know.

Ethics The *branch of philosophy* that examines what is right and wrong, good and bad, how people should live, and what they should do; also called moral philosophy.

Existentialism A view that questions the nature of existence, and emphasizes personal responsibility for choices.

Fallacy An error in *reasoning* that results in a false *statement*.

Falsification The process of testing a *theory* with the intent to prove it false.

Feminism The view that women should have the same rights as men.

Free expression The act of communicating our thoughts and *beliefs* without restrictions.

Free will The power to act by choice without being restricted by fate or by a superior force. See also *determinism*.

Freedom The ability to think, choose, and act for yourself, without restrictions.

Fundamental principle The *substance* or substances from which all things are made.

Generalization A broad *statement* based on a number of specific cases.

Hedonism The view that maximizing pleasure is the way to achieve human happiness.

Humanoid robot A machine designed with an artificial body that resembles that of a human.

Hypothesis A prediction made on limited evidence that is a starting point for further investigation.

Idealism The view that reality consists of *minds* and their ideas. The opposite is *materialism*.

Illusion A false *belief*, or a misinterpreted *perception* by one or more of the senses.

Induction The method of *reasoning* from past examples to reach a *conclusion* about the future. See also *deduction*.

Infinite Greater than any countable number, or impossible to measure.

Innate A quality or a feature that a person is born with naturally.

Just Fair according to an *innate* sense of what is right.

Justified Based on good reasons.

Knowledge A belief that must be at least both *true* and *justified*.

Liberty The *freedoms* given to people in a *society*.

Logic The branch of philosophy that studies *reasoning*, including how to construct a good *argument* and identify flaws in arguments.

Materialism The view that everything is made of *matter* (physical substances). The opposite is *idealism*.

Matter The physical *substance* that all things are made from.

Mental state The state of *mind* experienced by a person—their wishes, hopes, and emotions.

Metaphysics The *branch of philosophy* concerned with the fundamental nature of reality, identity, and existence.

Mind A person's inner thoughts, *beliefs*, experiences, and memories.

Mind–body dualism The view that humans are composed of a physical body, and a nonphysical *mind*.

Monism The view that something is formed of a single *substance*. See also *dualism*, *pluralism*.

Monotheism The *belief* that there is only one god.

Moral Concerned with standards of right and wrong, and good and bad behavior.

Moral relativism The view that what is right and wrong is not the same for everyone, and can change between cultures and between different periods in time.

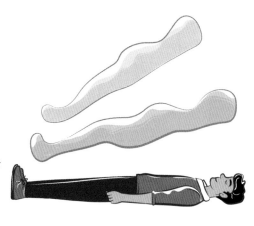

Morality Principles that determine right from wrong, as well as what is considered good or bad behavior.

Necessary Something that must be the case. The opposite is *contingent*.

Norm Something that is typical, usual, or an accepted standard or rule.

Noumena A "thing-in-itself" that exists independently of our experience, beyond the scope of our *minds*. The opposite is *phenomena*.

Objective Not influenced by emotions or opinions, but based on facts. The opposite is *subjective*.

Omnipotent Having great and unlimited power.

Paradox In *logic*, an *argument*, which, despite apparently sound *reasoning* from acceptable *premises*, leads to a *conclusion* that seems absurd.

Perceive The use of one or more of the five senses to gain awareness of things.

Perception An awareness of something, such as an object, physical sensation, or event, through the senses.

Perspectivism The view that there are no facts, only interpretations.

Phenomena The things that we experience, regardless of how things actually are in themselves. The opposite is *noumena*.

Philosophy of mind The *branch of philosophy* that studies the nature of consciousness, the *mind*, and the relationship of the mind to the physical body.

Physicalism The view that only physical things can possibly exist. See also *materialism*.

Pluralism The view that there are many types of thing. See also *dualism*, *monism*.

Political philosophy The *branch of philosophy* that examines the nature of *society* and the *state*, and *concepts* such as power, *freedom*, and equality.

Pragmatism A view that emphasizes the usefulness of *knowledge*: a *theory* or *belief* is successful if it can be practically applied.

Pre-Socratic Ancient Greek philosophy before Socrates, or Greek philosophy unaffected by his work.

Premise One of a group of *statements* in an *argument* from which a *conclusion* can be made.

Psychology The scientific (rather than philosophical) study of the human *mind* and its functions.

Rational Based on clear *reasoning*.

Rationalism The view that we can gain *knowledge* of the world through the use of *reasoning*, without relying on the experiences of our senses.

Reasoning The process of thinking about something in a structured and sensible way.

Represent To portray something in words or images.

Rights *Moral* and legal entitlements, such as food, shelter, and equal treatment.

Scholaticism A *school of philosophy* in the medieval period that sought to unite religious teachings with philosophical *reasoning*.

School of philosophy A set of philosophical beliefs shared by a group of people or philosophers.

Skepticism The philosophical position in which the possibility of *knowledge* is denied or doubted.

Society A group of people living together in an organized way according to agreed rules.

Solipsism The view that we can only be certain of our own existence, not the existence of other minds.

Soul The inner essence of something, often a human being. For some philosophers, the soul is a *substance*, and is believed to be immortal.

Sound In philosophy, a sound *argument* is one that is *valid* and that has true *premises*.

State (political) The political organization of *society*, including the institutions of government and the law.

Statement In *logic*, a sentence that can either be *true* or false.

Subjective Based on individual interpretation or personal taste. The opposite is *objective*.

Substance In philosophy, something that can exist without depending on anything else.

Synthetic truth A sentence that requires evidence to prove that it's true, e.g. "The building has six windows." The opposite is an *analytic truth*.

Theory An idea or a set of rules or principles that is used to explain a fact or event.

Thought experiment An imaginary scenario that allows a philosopher to fully explore a *concept* or *theory*.

Transcend To go beyond the range or limits of something.

True In accordance with fact or reality; genuine, accurate, or exact.

Universal Applies to everyone and everything, at all times.

Utilitarianism The view that the action that is *morally* right is the one that produces the most happiness.

Valid In *logic*, said of an *argument* in which the *conclusion necessarily* follows from the *premises*. If the premises are false, the conclusion may also be.

Virtue An excellent quality in a person, such as courage or honesty.

Virtuous Behavior that is considered to be good, or that shows high *moral* standards in accordance with *virtues*.

Zombie In philosophy, a person who seems like a human being, but who has no consciousness.

Index

INDEX

Acknowledgments

Dorling Kindersley would like to thank:
Mani Ramaswamy and Tayabah Khan for editorial assistance; Vishal Bhatia for DTP assistance; Vijay Kandwal and Nityanand Kumar for hi-res assistance; Harish Aggarwal, Priyanka Sharma, and Saloni Singh for the jacket.

(Key: a-above; b-below/bottom; c-center;
f-far; l-left; r-right; t-top)

ACKNOWLEDGMENTS